A
Storybook
Marriage

A Storybook Marriage

Forrest Pollock

TATE PUBLISHING & Enterprises

Published by Tate Publishing & Enterprises, LLC
127 E. Trade Center Terrace | Mustang, Oklahoma 73064 USA
1.888.361.9473 | www.tatepublishing.com

Tate Publishing is committed to excellence in the publishing industry. The company reflects the philosophy established by the founders, based on Psalm 68:11,
"The Lord gave the word and great was the company of those who published it."

Book design copyright © 2010 by Tate Publishing, LLC. All rights reserved.
Cover design by Blake Brasor
Interior design by Nathan Harmony

Published in the United States of America

ISBN: 978-1-60799-750-4
Religion: Christian Life: Love & Marriage
09.12.09

Dedications

Dearest Courtney, Brooke, Hope, Blake, and Kirk (Preston who went to be with our Lord).

I want you to know how much I love you and how much your father loved you.

Your daddy and I always wanted to demonstrate what a "storybook marriage" could be like. I know you never wondered whether your daddy and I loved each other or loved you.

My hope and prayer is that you children will find these pages to be helpful in your own search for a husband or wife and in your own marriage one day (In the far-distant future).

Each of you demonstrate the qualities of integrity and authenticity your father always desired for you to have ... I am so proud of you. "Walk in confidence that God is a rewarder of those who walk diligently and follow him" (Hebrews 11:6). Trust in God's faithfulness.

Acknowledgment

It is impossible for me to remember the thousands of you who have prayed, encouraged and cared for us during the huge loss in our lives. To all of you, "Thank you!"

Thank you to Dr. Timothy K. Christian, D.Min., Th.D., Interim Director, Mid-America Baptist Theological Seminar, Northeast Campus, Schenectady, NY who arranged the text of this book for Forrest from his sermons and sermon tapes.

A special thank you to my father, Dr. Loyd V. Allen, Jr., Ph.D., who helped me complete this book with the finishing touches. This book was completed just weeks before my husband and son died in a plane crash. As you know, there is a lot of work and time that goes into getting a book ready for the publisher. "Thank you, Daddy!"

I am grateful also to Barbie Frost, Jennifer Clark and George Thomason for answering endless emails and their encouragement to finish this book.

Also, thank you to Dr. Tom and Jeanie Elliff for your

pre-marital counseling, the surprise renewing of our vows on our tenth wedding anniversary, and eighteen years after our marriage, officiating at the funeral of my husband and son who went to be with our Father in Heaven. You gave us great counsel on having our storybook marriage.

Most importantly, to Bell Shoals Baptist Church of Brandon, Florida, who loved, cared and supports us (even now) during this very difficult time. We love and miss you so much: You will always be in our thoughts and prayers.

Table of Contents

Introduction

A little girl heard the story of "Snow White and the Seven Dwarfs." The fairytale has all the elements to thrill a little girl. There is a beautiful princess and a jealous, evil queen. There is a magic mirror and a poison apple. There are seven "vertically challenged" men, and of course, a handsome prince.

The girl excitedly told her mother the story. When she came to the part about the handsome prince awakening beautiful Snow White with a kiss, the little girl bubbled over with enthusiasm. "Mommy, do you know what happened next?"

Having been a little girl, of course mom knew; but she didn't want to spoil her daughter's joy in telling her story. So, after a pause she asked, "Did they live happily ever after?"

"Oh no, Mommy—*they got married!*"

Perhaps she was nearer the bull's eye than we would wish. "Happily ever after" is a great line in a storybook, but national statistics sadly tell a different story. The fact is, many marriages in America are in trouble. Divorce destroys at least half of our homes and Christians are not exempt. Couples who looked like Prince Charming and Snow White on their wedding day, end up acting like an evil troll and the wicked witch at their property division hearing. Fairytales become war stories. Little girls and boys are often collateral casualties.

This disturbing reality stirred my passion and birthed a dream. As the senior pastor of Bell Shoals Baptist Church in Brandon, Florida, I have a passion to encourage people; it motivates our church's motto as "The Fellowship of Encouragement."

In my pastoral ministry, I see many discouraged people. One of the greatest sources of discouragement is wounded and broken marriages. I dreamed of doing something about that. My dream was that we would experience a year without one couple in our 7,500-member congregation experiencing the devastation of divorce.

To be proactive, I tried to equip our people to experience marriage as God intended by delivering a series of messages in early 2007. The series apparently fed a hunger. Recordings of these sermons quickly became one of the most-requested series ever. Men and women wanted to hear them again and again, and share them with friends. That same passion and dream has now prompted me to preserve these messages in written form. They are the basis of this book.

We begin our story where most marriages begin: Dating. Starting right is the first step toward living happily ever after. We'll talk about it in Chapter 1: "Snow White and the Seven *Dorks*."

Chapter 2, "Beauty and the Beast," encourages you to build or, if necessary, *rebuild* your marriage on God's original foundation. Chapter 3, "Dumbo," tells you how to avoid five of the most foolish mistakes in marriage. Chapter 4, "Bedknobs and Boredstiff," suggests how you can rekindle romance in marriage. I wish Chapter 5 were not necessary. But it is. In "The Lying King," we will consider what to do when trust has been broken. Finally, Chapter 6, "Keeping Beauty," suggests steps you can take to keep the beauty in your marriage.

Join me in discovering *A Storybook Marriage* that is more than a fairy tale. Perhaps you and your mate will become the main characters.

—Dr. Forrest Pollock
Senior Pastor's Study
Bell Shoals Baptist Church
Summer 2008

Snow White and the Seven Dorks
Genesis 24

I proposed marriage to Miss Dawn Allen on our second date.

Could have done it sooner, but that would have been too sudden.

Needless to say, I was smitten. Her family used to tour the country singing Christian music, and one Sunday evening, they ministered at the church I attended. As a 26-year-old bachelor, then wondering if I would always be single, I eyed her from the second row. In fact, I couldn't take my eyes off her.

After the concert, we met briefly, but there were hundreds of young men vying for her attention. So what's a guy to do?

Call her up, that's what.

Unfortunately, without a telephone number, I had to call every "Allen" in the Oklahoma City phone book. At last, I found her father, Loyd. Thank heaven his name wasn't Zebedee.

To make a long story longer, she remembered me fondly and her parents gave us their blessing to go out.

From the first moment I met Dawn, I knew she was *the one*. For me, dating was a mere formality. In my heart, I knew we would be married. Thankfully, Dawn did too. (I learned later that she had told her father she had just met her future husband.)

As I was saying, my proposal came on the second date. Maybe I secretly feared what would happen if she *really* got to know me. In any event, during the six months before our wedding, her parents graciously permitted us to see each other twice each week, and one of those meetings had to be at church.

Since those days, I can honestly say we've had a storybook marriage. But while our story may be atypical, all storybook marriages begin in the same place. In fact, it's the same place a broken, miserable marriage begins: Dating.

Dating hasn't always been the norm. In eastern cultures even today, marriages are often arranged. In fact, arranged marriages were commonplace in Bible times. Case in point: Abraham arranged a marriage for his son Isaac. He sent a special servant to a special place to find a special woman among a special people.

Abraham's servant did not arrange a date; he arranged a marriage. But the way he went about finding a princess for his Prince Charming is illustrative for us today. The character of the mate Abraham's servant sought for Isaac is the kind of mate you should both seek, and seek to be.

If you are careful to begin with the right kind of *date*, you will end up with the right kind of *mate*.

Many Snow Whites wonder why their prince never comes. Could it be that they only date one of the seven dorks? I hope you will gain a clearer understanding of either how to avoid dating a dork or how to avoid being a dork yourself. (And by the way, guys are not always the problem. There are plenty of *dorkettes* out there too!)

Perhaps one clarification is in order: Marriage is not for everyone. No one is a second-class citizen if he or she remains single. Jesus was single. The prophets Jeremiah and Elijah were single. Mary, Martha and Lazarus were all single. Indeed, the apostle Paul noted the advantages of singleness. He praised the high calling of a life exclusively devoted to Christ, in 1 Corinthians 7, as a gift. So remember this: Mathematicians teach that ONE is a *whole number*. If you are single and content... to God be the glory! It is far better to be a satisfied single, than to be miserably married.

If, however, you desire to marry or remarry, begin with this thought:

You will someday marry someone you date.

Therefore, it is vital for you get dating right. You do not have to go out with every one of the seven dorks to find your Prince Charming.

The Assignment

Abraham lived 2,000 years before Christ's birth. Though he didn't realize it at the time, he was one of the most influential men in world history.

Abraham was in the autumn of life. Yet God had promised to give him an enormous family. He believed God's promise,[1] but for Abraham's family to multiply, it had to begin. So it was time to find a wife for his beloved son Isaac.

As Genesis 24 tells the story, Abraham summoned his chief servant and made him take an oath:

> "I want you to find a wife for my son," Abraham said. "But be careful about where you find her. Plenty of idol worshipers are around here. Some of them even practice child sacrifices. None of these women will make the right kind of daughter-in-law or wife. Instead, go back to my home country and find a woman among my relatives who worship my God."

When we swear an oath in court, we place a left hand on the Bible and raise a right hand in a solemn promise "to tell the truth, the whole truth, and nothing but the truth, so help me God." Abraham's servant took an equally solemn and binding oath. The servant placed his hand under Abraham's thigh (that's how they did it in Old Testament days).[2] And now the search was on.

The Search

As Abraham's servant went looking for "Mrs. Right," we discover seven keys for finding the prince or princess of your dreams.

First, if you are single but desperately desire to be married, I have two words for you ...

Chill Out

Isaac was forty years old when Dad finally arranged his marriage (Genesis 25:20). He was an old bachelor. But we see no evidence that Isaac was anxious that his biological clock was ticking.

How about you? Are you concerned that you're not married? Take a deep breath. *Relax.* Marriage is too important a decision to rush. If you date and then marry the wrong person, you will live with the significant, negative, and lasting consequences of that decision for the rest of your life. And as the old Johnny Mathis song says, "that's a long, long time."

Have you ever gone to a favorite restaurant when you were famished? The hostess asks, "Do you want smoking, nonsmoking, or first-available?" If you are a non-smoker, you are faced with a dilemma. You see a long list of people ahead of you. Hunger clouds your judgment. "First available!" you say. Soon you are called, ahead of people who were waiting when you arrived. You feel proud of yourself, even a little smug, and of course, you are seated amidst billowing clouds of puffy smoke. "It'll be okay," you reassure yourself. But your eyes start to water. Your nose gets itchy. Nevertheless, your stomach assures you that you made the right choice. You order. The food comes. You eat enough to calm your hunger pangs, but now you realize you messed up. Why? Because you settled. What should have given you great delight, has given you great dissatisfaction.

Chill out. Don't become obsessed with being married. Anxiety will make you settle. You don't want to be like the singles who are so love-hungry, they will accept the first Tom,

Dick, or Mary who comes along. As Dr. Laura says, "They become beggars, not choosers" in the dating process.

The Apostle Paul wrote, "I have learned to be content whatever the circumstances" (Philippians 4:11). How about you? Have you learned contentment?

In essence, Paul says chill out. He cautions, "Do not look for a wife" (1 Corinthians 7:27b NIV).

But you ask, "How will I ever find my Snow White if I don't look for her?" Or, "How will I locate my handsome prince if I'm not on the prowl?"

Try this instead: *focus on being the right person rather than finding the right person*. Matthew 6:33 says, "Seek first his kingdom and his righteousness, and all these things will be given to you as well." If you will " ... delight yourself in the LORD ... he will give you the desires of your heart" (Psalm 37:4 NIV).

Remember, God has the very hairs of your head numbered (Matthew 10:30). And if God is concerned about minutia such as tallying the number of hairs on your head, you can be confident your heavenly Father is far more concerned about the man or woman with whom you will spend the rest of your life.

A second thing you can do is ...

Trust Your Heavenly Father

Why not let your heavenly Father bring your spouse to you? Notice, father Abraham took the initiative in scoping out a wife for his son. Did you know that you can trust your Father to do the same? The Bible says, "Trust in the LORD with all your heart and lean not on your own understanding" (Proverbs 3:5 NIV).

Sometimes I ask single girls, "What kind of guy would you like to marry?" The answer is usually something like this: "I want a husband who is six feet four, has Ashton Kutcher's face, Adonis' body, and Donald Trump's money."

Time passes and as she turns her reliance upon God to bring her the husband He has for her, the call finally comes: "Pastor, you won't believe it!" she gushes. "God has answered my prayers. It was amazing. I did what you suggested. I focused on 'being' instead of 'finding.' And God brought me the man of my dreams." Change to read: ": ... "

Then I see the guy she found. He may fulfill her dreams and be all she desired but he may also be pudgy, have a poor complexion and drive a Yugo. But in her eyes, he is a Prince Charming. Did she settle? No way! She let her Father orchestrate a whole series of unlikely events that brought them together to live happily ever after.

You can let God do the heavy lifting for you as well. Focus on being the right person instead of seeking the right person. Trust God to introduce your spouse to you at just the right time. His choice will be best. He will not pair you with a dork.

Our heavenly Father, I believe, often uses our earthly fathers to run interference for their children. Dads, one of your jobs is to protect your kids from dorks.

We have three beautiful daughters, Courtney, Brooke, and Hope. They take after their Mom in the looks department, so when they are old enough to date, I suspect there will be no shortage of eager young men. Therefore, we have already agreed on how the dating process will work at our house. When a boy asks one of our girls out, they have agreed to respond, "You'll have to ask my Dad." Then I spring into action to fulfill my God-given role as a dork-filter.

If Bubba has enough guts to present himself to me (while I'm sharpening a bowie knife)... then, I *might* let him take my precious darling out, but not until I have a chance to discern his true intentions and take measure of his character and Christian walk. Without getting to know the young man, I feel my negligence might put a Stradivarius violin in the hands of a gorilla.

Young ladies, has some knucklehead ever asked you out, and you said yes only because you didn't want to hurt his feelings? You can admit it now; it was a nightmare, right? Have your former friends set you up with blind dates before, but failed to mention key facts, such as that the guy has lazy eye... and he is seeing somebody else on the side? Wouldn't you agree that "dork" accurately describes what you got?

How can you avoid being caught in the dork trap? It's simple. Use your father, an older brother, or a trustworthy uncle to run interference for you. Then, you can honestly say, "Sorry, but he won't let me go." Case closed.

Believe me; I have no problem telling a dork to get lost. I will be happy to take the heat. My daughters are too precious to me to do otherwise.

A third consideration is to...

Look for Love in the Right Places

Notice, Abraham admonished his servant not to "get a wife for my son from the daughters of the Canaanites, among whom I am living, but go to my country and my own relatives and get a wife for my son Isaac" (Genesis 24:3b-4 NIV).

The lesson is this: Look for love in the *right* places. Be discerning about where you search for a spouse. I found mine in church—I can't think of a better place, can you? Don't look for a wife at some seedy honky-tonk or the Crystal Pistol. You don't find diamonds in a pigpen.

By the way, while we are talking about the *right* places to look for love, let's mention a few *wrong* places to go when you are on a date...

If you spend too much one-on-one time with your boyfriend or girlfriend, you will eventually run out of things to talk about, and then you are flirting with disaster. Never go to someone's house or apartment if his or her parents are gone. Don't make exceptions, such as, "My folks will be back in a little while," or "We won't do anything except watch TV." Rationalizations lead to regrets—and the regrets may be irreversible. Don't do it!

Yes, this is mainly wisdom for teenagers, but some adults would be wise to heed the same advice. All should avoid the appearance of evil and it may protect you from the acts of evil. Run together and go places with a group of friends. There is safety in numbers. There is purity in numbers as well.

Those are pastoral concerns. Now back to the Bible...

¹⁰Then the servant took ten of his master's camels and left, taking with him all kinds of good things from his master. He set out for Aram Naharaim and made his way to the town of Nahor. ¹¹He had the camels kneel down near the well outside the town; it was toward evening, the time the women go out to draw water.

Genesis 24:10–11

Abraham sent his servant to a *special place* to a *special people*, looking for a *special person* for a *special purpose*. You, too, can trust your Heavenly Father to lead you to your future spouse at just the right time. So in review, first, chill out. Second, trust your Father. Third, look for love in the right places among the right people. And now, fourth…

Profile in Prayer

Notice the chief servant's prayer:

> Then he prayed, "O LORD, God of my master Abraham, give me success today, and show kindness to my master Abraham. See, I am standing beside this spring, and the daughters of the townspeople are coming out to draw water. May it be that when I say to a girl, 'Please let down your jar that I may have a drink,' and she says, 'Drink, and I'll water your camels too' [*This woman did not fear work. A camel can drink twenty-one gallons of water in ten minutes,³ and she was watering a caravan of ten camels* (Gen. 24:10 NIV)*! Evidently, she valued service and hospitality.*]—let her be the one you have chosen

for your servant Isaac. By this I will know that you have shown kindness to my master.

Genesis 24:12–14 (NIV)

The servant prayed and then he profiled Isaac's wife-to-be with prayer. Profiling your ideal spouse is a great idea.

Profiling can be done through prayer and fasting, sharing your desires with God and trusting Him for the best answer at the best time. You have no right to dictate to God, but you have every right to ask of God. He invites you, because of Jesus Christ, to "approach the throne of grace with confidence" (Hebrews 4:16). Your heavenly Father will fulfill your desires or change your desires. Either way will be awesome. You can trust Him.

I am suggesting a tried and proven method. It worked for Abraham's servant and it worked for me. Just before I met my wife Dawn, I had a long conversation in prayer with the Heavenly Father. I was twenty-six years old and did not know if He had someone for me. In prayer, I profiled the kind of woman I wanted if God should choose to give me a wife. I prayed it and wrote it down. First, I asked for a Christian woman. Next, I wanted her to love children, music, and me. I identified several other traits too, all of which were wonderfully embodied in Dawn. In fact, if you look closely at her wedding ring, she has a multi-stone setting. Each stone represents a specific trait God gave her that was a specific answer to my prayer.

If you do not know who you are looking for, how will you know when you find "the one"? If you are desperate or starved for love, you may compromise your standards and settle for the first available warm body. You don't want to fall into the "I've-Gotta-Have-Somebody" Syndrome.

Instead of being desperate, you can be discerning. A suggested, bare minimum, profile should include at least four characteristics:

Christian

First, a prospective date and mate should be a Christian. Does the young man, or woman, have a personal testimony and a changed lifestyle?

Someone who knows Jesus Christ will be able to point to a certain time in life when he or she personally trusted Jesus Christ as Lord and Savior. A Christian makes a conscious decision to repent of sin and to trust and follow Jesus Christ. A genuine believer will not be embarrassed to talk about his or her faith in, and walk with, the Lord Jesus Christ.

A Christian has a changed lifestyle. Do not be fooled by someone who says, "I'm a Christian, but I don't go to church." Attending church does not make a person a Christian. But a Christian wants to hang out with other Christians. Christians hunger for the comfort and encouragement and spiritual food found in a Bible-believing, Christ-honoring, joy-filled church family.

Faithful Christians also value sexual purity. They *do not* take advantage of the people they date. Further, they desire to study, pray, and apply the Scriptures to their lives. They forgive others because they have received abundant forgiveness from God. Their lifestyle reflects a life-transforming relationship with Jesus Christ.

Remember: *You will eventually marry somebody you date.* Don't waste your time with *dorks* that are unsaved. Your heavenly Father has already told you *not* to marry an unsaved person. So, don't even agree to a recreational date. Why? *You will defraud your date.* How? Dating declares, "I'm interested in you, and I may become even more interested." If you give a false impression, you defraud the other person.

I have often declared from my pulpit, "Do not be unequally yoke together with unbelievers" (2 Corinthians 6:14 NIV), and that admonition includes marrying an unbeliever. Yet, people still ask, "Is it okay to date an unsaved person?" Girls will say, "But pastor, no Christian guys ever ask me out. And besides, I'm going to witness to him. If he tries to kiss me, I'll press a Bible to his lips!"

I applaud their evangelistic fervor, but I question their wisdom. "Missionary dating" leads to an inordinate number of false professions. Why? Because guys will do anything (yes, anything!) to impress a girl. If a guy needs to walk an aisle, be baptized, speak in tongues, bark, laugh, or lick lint out of Buddha's belly button, he will do it to keep a girl. Many of you are wondering, "Are all guys that conniving and deceptive?" Candidly, Yes!

The "logic" behind the missionary approach to dating is disturbing. Do you honestly believe you can establish a healthy relationship based on a hidden agenda? Isn't it slightly dishonest and disingenuous to misrepresent your motivation and deceive another person? When you recognize spiritual incompatibility with a potential date, stay out of the relationship. If you are already in such a dating relationship, get out.

Trying to change another person is one of the most foolish things one can ever attempt. You are responsible for your behavior. You cannot control another person; you can only accept another person as he or she is. There's an old saying, "You can't teach a pig how to sing¾you'll only frustrate yourself and irritate the pig." It is not your job to change, mold, heal, fix, or reform the person you date. The most foolish thought of all is, "I'll change him after we are married."

If you cannot connect with someone on a spiritual level, your relationship is doomed. What you believe about God, how you pray, where you worship, the holidays you celebrate, the books you hold to be sacred, and your opinion on baptism are just a few of the things that make up your spiritual belief system. Find someone who shares those beliefs. Find a Christian.

Second, look for...

Chemistry/Compatibility

A common chemistry with a potential date is imperative because you are a tripartite being—body, soul, and spirit (1 Thessalonians 5:23 NIV). There should be a recognizable chemistry on all three levels. Two Christians can have a spiritual chemistry; you can have a common love for, and bond in, Jesus Christ. But, just because somebody is a good prayer partner does not mean he or she would make a good spouse.

There should be a physical chemistry as well. Ask yourself, "Am I attracted to this person physically?" When

Isaac saw Rebekah, he obviously thought she was drop-dead gorgeous. There is nothing wrong with that. Beauty and attractiveness are in the eye of the beholder. If you are to be the "beholder" for the rest of your life, the person you date should be attractive *to you*. Is there a physical chemistry between you?

I do not mind telling you, I think my wife is a knock-out. I look at her and my motor starts running. Our physical chemistry has grown, rather than diminished, through the years of our marriage.

Dawn and I also have a soul-chemistry between us. We agree about how day-to-day family life should happen. We share common convictions and common goals. Our outlook on life is amazingly similar. Our souls are in tune. Certainly there are differences between us. Someone rightly said, "When two people agree on everything, one of them is unnecessary." Dawn and I do have differences, but the similarities far outweigh them.

When you consider dating someone, ask yourself, "Do we really have much in common? Do we like the same things? Do we have similar tastes? Do we share common convictions?"

The "opposites attract" relationship works great on the big screen, but in reality, it is extremely tough to pull off. In the healthiest relationships, the similarities far outweigh the differences. Do you share a body, soul, and spiritual oneness?

Remember this: Before marriage, opposites *attract*. After marriage, opposites *irritate*.

And that leads us to a third characteristic in your minimum profile...

You may be attracted to someone, but can you get along? Or do you fight like ally cats? Also, ask yourself if you can get along with your sweetheart's family? The old saying is true, "The apple doesn't fall far from the tree." Chances are, if you can't get along with the family, you won't get along with your sweetheart because, generally speaking, your date will turn out like his or her parents. That was one reason Abraham demanded that his servant make a B-line to his family's hometown. He knew a woman with a similar background would have the greatest potential of being compatible with Isaac.

Abraham's servant prayed, and God answered. "Before he had finished praying, Rebekah came out with her jar on her shoulder. She was the daughter of Bethuel son of Milcah, who was the wife of Abraham's brother Nahor" (Genesis 24:15 NIV).

The fourth characteristic in your minimum profile is...

Character

Verse 16 adds, "The girl was very beautiful, a *virgin* [emphasis mine]; no man had ever lain with her."

Rebekah was a girl of character. She had kept herself pure. But without divine revelation or offensive questions that you have no business asking early in a relationship, how can you discern the character of a potential spouse? Several suggestions may be helpful.

Look at his or her friends. What kind of people hang out with your date? Friends are a window into a person's character. We gravitate toward those with whom we have most in common. Furthermore, we become mosaics of our associates. The apostle Paul said, "Do not be misled: 'Bad company corrupts good character'" (1 Corinthians 15:33 NIV). Rarely does the influence flow the other way. A guy who hangs out with dorks either is a dork or is on the way to becoming one.

Pay attention to how they treat their parents, siblings, or teachers. If they disrespect them, they will disrespect you.

Look at their honesty. If that guy or girl will lie about little things, he or she will lie about big things. Bank on it, invest in it, and reap the dividends. *Can your date make a commitment?* Can he hold a job longer than a week? Does she keep her promises to you and to others?

How does he or she respond to pressure? Tough times reveal character. Crises will be revealing.

How do they treat you in private? Does respect grow or disappear when no one is watching? *Character is who you are when you're alone.*

The fifth principle for finding the prince or princess of your dreams is remembering that your body belongs to God. So ...

Practice Purity

Rebekah understood that. She was a virgin (v. 16). She did not go to bed with a man until she married her husband. Her wedding night was a sacred unveiling.

Grace allows me to encourage those who have failed in this area. I want you to know you can be forgiven. The blood of Jesus Christ cleanses all sin (1 John 1:7 NIV).

Look at Jesus Christ's response to a woman who had been sexually promiscuous. Jesus went out of his way to meet the woman at the well (John 4:4 NIV). She had been divorced five times and was shacking up with a sixth man. Yet, amazingly, Jesus, holy God in the flesh, did not *condemn* her. But notice, neither did He *condone* her actions. Instead, He told her where she could find living water. "Where sin increased, grace increased all the more" (Romans 5:20 NIV).

In contrast, some religious Nazis caught a woman in the very act of adultery. They threw her naked into the dirty streets to be stoned to death, but Jesus didn't join in. Instead, He stooped down and wrote in the sand. The mob grew quiet as Jesus looked at her, and said to them, "Anyone here who has never sinned can throw the first stone" (John 8:7 NIV). Everyone backed off. The only one who had never sinned passed on the opportunity; He left the stone in the street. Instead, Jesus said to her, "You may go now, but don't sin anymore" (John 8:10–11 NIV).

If you will genuinely repent of sexual sin, you will be spiritually renewed. In God's eyes, you will be like a virgin again. He will not cast the first stone. Instead, He will cast your sin into the depths of the sea of His forgiveness (Micah 7:19 NIV).

Please do not misinterpret my encouragement. Grace is not an invitation to sin; it is an opportunity for repentance and restoration. From this day forward, commit your body to God.

"You were bought at a price. Therefore honor God with your body" (1 Corinthians 6:20 NIV). That means you can and you must refrain from "physical intimacy" until you have exchanged wedding rings at the marriage altar.

First Corinthians 6:19 NIV reads, "Your body is a temple of the Holy Spirit…you are not your own." The only ones who have the right to share your temple are God and your spouse. *Period.*

Society's party line on sex is simple: Everybody's Doing It. From Abercrombie & Fitch catalogs, TV bimbos, to your classmates at school; it's easy to get the impression that everyone is having sex. Recent surveys, however, show this is sheer nonsense. Millions of young people *are* saving their bodies for marriage. The Centers for Disease Control reported that 54.4 percent of teens are abstaining from sex. Another recent study discovered that the virginity rate among teens steadily rose over the last decade. The truth is, everybody is *not* doing it.

Inevitably, someone asks, "How far can a Christian go?" The very question reveals that someone is on a slippery slope. Young people ask if it is okay to hold hands or to kiss. My stock answer is, *if you arouse passions you cannot biblically fulfill, you have gone too far.*

For some, simply holding hands or a kiss on the cheek arouses passions that cannot be biblically fulfilled. If you are one of those people, don't do it. It may be hard to believe, but I have performed more than one wedding where the kiss at the marriage altar was the bride and groom's first kiss.

I know what some young lady is thinking. "If I don't get physical with him, he'll leave." To that, I say…

"Fine—let him leave! Dump him!"

The fact is, if you allow a guy to have his way with you, he will never respect you. You see, what guys really want is a challenge. When you become physically intimate with a man, he is no longer on the hunt. Guys stop chasing a streetcar once they've caught it. So be bold and say, "No." You will not only earn his respect; you will hold his interest.

By the way, ladies, this applies to dress. Exercise modesty. Many young ladies don't understand the way God wired guys, and they unwittingly seduce men with their revealing clothing. Remember this: Guys are turned on by what they see. If you dress as if you are auditioning for an MTV video, you send the wrong message. Girls, be smart and dress like a lady, not like a tramp. Don't arouse passions you cannot biblically fulfill.

In his classic book, *The Art of War*, Sun Tzu said, "*Every battle is won before it is ever fought.*" In other words, winning any battle is all about preparation. The decisions you make before you get into the heat of battle give you the victory.

The same applies to sex and sexual purity. Carefully calculated decisions are never made in the heat of passion. The commitment to purity must be made in advance of passion. Please determine today not to give your body away until you are married. Today's commitment will help you stay pure until that special dayPractice purity. It is the fifth principle for finding the prince or princess of your dreams.

Sixth, watch for …

Red Flags

Abraham's servant did. He carefully scoped out Rebekah. He did reconnaissance.

> The servant hurried to meet her and said, "Please give me a little water from your jar."
>
> "Drink, my lord," she said, and quickly lowered the jar to her hands and gave him a drink.
>
> After she had given him a drink, she said, "I'll draw water for your camels too, until they have finished drinking." So she quickly emptied her jar into the trough, ran back to the well to draw more water, and drew enough for all his camels. *Without saying a word, the man watched her closely* [emphasis mine] to learn whether or not the LORD had made his journey successful.
>
> When the camels had finished drinking, the man took out a gold nose ring weighing a beka and two gold bracelets weighing ten shekels. Then he asked, "Whose daughter are you? Please tell me, is there room in your father's house for us to spend the night?"
>
> She answered him, "I am the daughter of Bethuel, the son that Milcah bore to Nahor." And she added, "We have plenty of straw and fodder, as well as room for you to spend the night."
>
> Genesis 24:17–25 (NIV)

Why did Abraham's servant watch Rebekah closely (v. 21)? Why did he ask about her family (v. 23)? He wanted to be sure God had really answered his prayer (v. 21). She fit part of the profile, but what about the rest of his prayer?

After all, she arrived before he said "Amen" (v. 15). Could God really answer that quickly? He wanted to be sure no red flags indicated her arrival was only a coincidence. He wanted God's confirmation.

Certain red flags give sufficient warning that a date would not likely make a good mate. Allow me to suggest three of these red flags.

Abuse

First, any form of abuse you experience is a serious red flag. There is no reasonable explanation for abuse—ever. I'm astonished at the efforts people make to justify abuse, especially when the abused person offers the justifications: "He didn't mean it" or "He's under a lot of stress." And the scariest response of all: "It's all right because I know it will never happen again." Don't bet on it! If he lays a hand on you, get away from him *now*. If he abuses you when you are dating, what would he do if you were married? If he abuses you, what would he do to your crying child? Run *now*! Run *far*! Run *fast*!

Second, be on the lookout for the red flag of...

Addictions

By their very nature, addictions are powerful habits. They are not easily overcome. If you date an addict, you are dealing with a person in bondage. A healthy relationship is utterly impossible. The drug, whatever its form, is that person's number one priority. Your handsome prince will always have a mistress. You will always be second, third, or lower in his priorities.

A third red flag is a bad ...

Attitude

Does your sweetheart have a real problem with authority? Does he "talk back" to his parents, coaches or teachers? Does she think it is cool to belittle others? If so, it won't be long before you are in the crosshairs of their criticism, and Rodney Dangerfield won't be the only one who "don't get no respect."

Abraham's servant observed her closely. He asked pertinent questions. He confirmed there were no red flags. And then and only then did he move from wondering to worshiping.

> Then the man bowed down and worshiped the Lord, saying, "Praise be to the Lord, the God of my master Abraham, who has not abandoned his kindness and faithfulness to my master. As for me, the Lord has led me on the journey to the house of my master's relatives."
>
> Genesis 24:26–27 (NIV)

Ask Crucial Questions

Finally, to find the prince or princess of your dreams, ask some crucial questions. Notice how Genesis 24 progresses.

Rebekah rushed home to tell her family about Abraham's servant. She showed them the jewelry he had given. Laban, her older brother, went to the spring to escort the caravan back to their home.

> So the man went to the house, and the camels were unloaded. Straw and fodder were brought for the camels, and water for him and his men to wash their feet. Then food was set before him, but he said, "I will not eat until I have told you what I have to say."
> "Then tell us," Laban said.
>
> Genesis 24:32–33

The servant recounted how God had blessed Abraham with great wealth (v. 35). He noted that Isaac was the son of Abraham and Sarah's old age, and all of Abraham's wealth was willed to Isaac (v. 36). This assured the family that Isaac could properly provide for Rebekah. He explained why Abraham had sent him, how God had led him to the right place and the right people, and how God had confirmed that Rebekah was the woman for Isaac. Then, "50Laban and Bethuel [Rebekah's older brother and Dad] answered, "This is from the LORD; we can say nothing to you one way or the other. 51Here is Rebekah; take her and go, and let her become the wife of your master's son, as the LORD has directed." (Genesis 34–51 select verses)

Rebekah's family concluded this was a match made in heaven. Family approval was enthusiastically given.

Of course, you are wondering how you can make the same determination today. How can you know that a relationship is truly of the Lord? At least *four crucial questions* should be answered before making or accepting a marriage proposal. First, answer the ...

Freedom Question

Do we have scriptural freedom to marry? Two passages note God's often overlooked parameters for marriage and remarriage.

> By law a married woman is bound to her husband as long as he is alive, but if her husband dies, she is released from the law of marriage. So then, if she marries another man while her husband is still alive, she is called an adulteress. But if her husband dies, she is released from that law and is not an adulteress, even though she marries another man.
>
> Romans 7:2–3 (NIV)

> If a woman has a husband who is not a believer and he is willing to live with her, she must not divorce him.... But if the unbeliever leaves, let him do so. A believing man or woman is not bound in such circumstances; God has called us to live in peace.... Nevertheless, each one should retain the place in life that the Lord assigned to him and to which God has called him. This is the rule I lay down in all the churches.
>
> 1 Corinthians 7:13, 15, 17 (NIV)

The freedom question must be answered. Do both the husband and wife have the scriptural freedom to marry?

Obviously, if neither of you has been previously married, you have scriptural freedom to marry. If you have been married before, but your spouse died, you have scriptural freedom. Likewise, if you were the victim of adultery or physical abandonment, then you have freedom to marry.

But note: some people do not have scriptural freedom to marry. Just because you are single does not mean you have the right to marry. So be careful here. Search the scriptures, pray, and see if it is God's will for you to marry again. It may be that the Lord desires for you to reconcile with your first spouse rather than try marriage again. Remember, if God forbids a relationship, what makes you think God would bless the relationship?

Second, ask the...

Family Question

Do both families enthusiastically encourage the marriage?

Abraham obviously blessed Isaac and Rebekah's marriage. He arranged it. The servant secured the blessing of Rebekah's family. He would not proceed without it. You, likewise, need both sets of parents to bless your marriage. Otherwise, every crisis in your marriage (and there will be some) may be met with, "See, I told you so. You never should have married him."

If both you and your sweetheart's parents are believers, yet they have serious reservations about you two getting married, do not ignore this huge red flag.

So serious is the matter of parental encouragement that I will not perform a wedding if any parent voices an objection before the ceremony. Even if the gown has been ordered and Dad has already paid the bill; I will not perform the wedding. Even if the cake has been made and delivered; I will not do it. Even if the limo is idling in the parking lot¾ I refuse to ignore this huge red flag waving before the marriage altar.

Let your parents be God's last red flag, lest you live to regret it later. Always ask for your parents' blessing before you get married.

Third, answer the...

Financial Question

Can the *husband alone* financially support the family?

Isaac had a substantial inheritance. Rebekah's family had the assurance he could care for her. You probably do not have the luxury of a large inheritance. So, how will you live? Neither the power company, the grocery store, nor your cell phone service will negotiate a deal that allows you to live on love.

The husband should take responsibility for supporting his household. Now don't get bent out of shape—-there is nothing sinful about a woman working outside the home. The ideal woman in Proverbs 31 was a working girl. But let the wife's income provide for luxuries—the vacation, the second car, and other non-essentials. Let the man's income pay for food, clothing, and shelter. If God should bless you with a baby, or the wife just wants to quit working, the devil will try to find a toehold in your relationship by throwing you into financial crisis. The fact is, financial pressure is the leading cause of divorce in America by a four-to-one margin.

Fourth, and most importantly, answer the ...

Faith Question

Are you both born again and attending the same church? Nations fight wars over religious differences. Do not imagine faith questions can be peacefully ignored in your home. A truce may be successfully maintained until your first child arrives, but then the battle lines will be drawn. Your heavenly father wants to unite your home. Heed His loving warning: "Do not be yoked together with unbelievers. For what do righteousness and wickedness have in common? Or what fellowship can light have with darkness?" (2 Corinthians 6:14 NIV).

The story in Genesis 24 continues. The freedom, family, financial, and faith questions were successfully answered. Only one question remained. The family "called Rebekah and asked her, 'Will you go with this man?'"

"I will go," she said (v. 58).

With God's confirmation and her family's blessing, verse 67 says, "Isaac brought her into the tent of his mother Sarah, and he married Rebekah. So she became his wife, and he loved her.

Another marriage in the gook of Genesis involved Adam and Eve. From this special relationship, we will study companionship, cooperation and commitment in the next chapter.

Beauty and the Beast
Genesis 2

Genesis 2 unfolds the story of the first marriage in true storybook fashion. God brought the first woman, Eve, to the first man, Adam. God himself gave the bride to the groom, then he performed the first wedding ceremony. Eve was a beautiful damsel. Adam was a handsome prince. Theirs was a storybook marriage. Adam and Eve were truly a match made in heaven, but they were polar opposites. That's why I entitled this chapter, *Beauty and The Beast*.

Adam and Eve were different from any other family in many ways. For example, they had no money problems, health problems, or in-law problems. No one competed for their affections. Eve never told Adam about all the other men she *could have* married. Adam could honestly say, "Baby, there's no one else in the world for me but you."

Certain things were different for Adam and Eve, yet some things are perpetually the same. Eternal truths in the story of the first family can help you have a happy and healthy marriage today. The first marriage is instructive for every marriage. Notice three unchanging truths about marriage.

The Purpose of Marriage: Companionship

First, the purpose of marriage has not changed. Marriage was and is for companionship. Notice, The Lord God said, "It is not good for the man to be alone. I will make a helper suitable for him."(Genesis 2:18 NIV).

God gave marriage and the home to meet humankind's deepest emotional, physical, psychological, and spiritual needs. Adam desired a physical, human companion with whom he could fellowship. None of the animals would do. Genesis 2:19–20 NIV states:

> Now the LORD God had formed out of the ground all the beasts of the field and all the birds of the air. He brought them to the man to see what he would name them; and whatever the man called each living creature, that was its name. So the man gave names to all the livestock, the birds of the air and all the beasts of the field.

Why did God give Adam the job of naming animals? Could God not think of any names Himself? Of course He could! God had a purpose. He used the assignment to create a desire in Adam's heart.

Imagine. First, a large gray animal with floppy ears and a long snout approached. Adam stroked his chin and said, "Yep, that's an elephant." Next! A big creature with short legs and a huge mouth presented itself. "That's a hippopotamus," Adam said. And then a skunk¾what else would you call a skunk, but a skunk?

Adam named all the animals on earth. As he did he observed, *because this was back when men were observant*, that for Mr. Giraffe, there was a Mrs. Giraffe. For Mr. Hippo, there was Mrs. Hippo, only she didn't want be called that. Even for Mr. Skunk, there was Mrs. Skunk. But for Mr. Adam, there was no Mrs. Adam. The last part of Genesis 2:20 is almost sad, "But for Adam no suitable helper was found." Now we are ready for the rest of the story.

God is good. Having created the desire in Adam, God satisfied that desire. He created a woman and brought her to Adam.

> So the LORD God caused the man to fall into a deep sleep; and while he was sleeping, he took one of the man's ribs and closed up the place with flesh. Then the LORD God made a woman from the rib he had taken out of the man, and he brought her to the man.

Adam approved. In fact, he was thrilled. He said:
"This is now bone of my bones and flesh of my flesh; she shall be called 'woman,'
   for she was taken out of man."

Adam's statement was a poetic exclamation. He reveled in finding his counterpart, the one who was like him. Basically, his words about bones and flesh mean, "Wow!" Adam had seen all of the other creatures. He gave them appropriate names. But when he saw Eve he said, "Hubba hubba!"

Don't miss the enormity of Adam and Eve's companionship. Adam had been face-to-face, one-on-one, with Almighty God. God personally visited Adam in the Garden of Eden; they walked and talked every afternoon. Adam's deepest spiritual needs were fully satisfied. Yet, amazingly, something was missing in his heart; an unmet need remained. Eve was tailor-made to satisfy Adam's God-created need for human companionship.

Marriage is intended to be the highest, the holiest, the deepest, and most satisfying of all human relationships. That's why Genesis 2:24 NIV says, "For this reason a man will leave his father and mother and be united to his wife, and they will become one flesh." The relationship between husband and wife is to be a closer and stronger bond than the one between you and your parents or you and your children.

First, the purpose of marriage is companionship. God said, "It is not good that the man should be alone." is intended to meet the deepest emotional, spiritual, physical and psychological earthly needs of a husband and wife.

The Partnership of Marriage: Cooperation

If the purpose of marriage is being fulfilled, the partnership of marriage will be enjoyed. True companionship will lead to a delightful cooperation. Notice the second part of Genesis 2:18 (HCSB), "The LORD God said, 'It is not good for the man to be alone. I will make a helper suitable for him.'"

A "helper suitable" means "a helper who is like him" (HCSB). Woman was created to be a partner who perfectly corresponded to man. They shared the same nature. What Adam lacked, Eve supplied. What Eve lacked, Adam supplied.[1] We sometimes laughingly call our husbands or our wives "the other half." Actually, this is appropriate. Adam without Eve was like a violin without a bow.

God gave Eve to Adam to make up the part of Adam that was lacking. She was his *completer*, not his *competer*.

Today, political correctness has run amuck. On many fronts, the battle of the sexes has escalated into full-scale war. Men and women compete rather than cooperate. But this is not God's original plan.

God's plan was infinitely superior, and He perfectly executed His plan. God performed the first surgery. He administered anesthesia, placing Adam in a "deep sleep" (Genesis 2:21 NIV). God then removed one of Adam's ribs, perhaps with some surrounding flesh,[2] and used it as the raw material to make woman. The Hebrew word translated "woman" in verses 22 and 23, is *ishah*. The word translated "man" is *ish*. The *ishah* was made out of the rib of the *ish*; she was literally "bone of my bones and flesh of my flesh ... for she was taken out of man" (verse 23).

Significantly, *ishah*, "woman," comes from a root meaning *to be soft*.[3] God built femininity into women. The word *ish*, "man," comes from a root meaning *to exercise power*. God put masculinity in man. God made them different so that He might make them "one."

Have you seen the informative book, *Everything Men Know About Women*? The back of the book promises that, "based on years of research and interviews with thousands of men from all walks of life," the reader will discover "the most complete picture ever revealed of men's knowledge of the opposite sex." With this and other profound promises, many hopeful men have opened the book to discover … every page is blank.

Men and women are inherently, and sometimes mysteriously different. But don't misunderstand¾different does not mean either inferior or superior. Our God-created differences enhance our companionship and cooperation.

The best partnerships are between two people who bring different strengths and different weaknesses to the relationship. The last thing a business partnership needs is for both people to have the same weaknesses and strengths. If both are the same, one partner is unnecessary, and so it is in marriage.

Why then are some feminists trying to move heaven and earth to prove there are no differences between men and women? Sometimes their efforts are just plain silly.

———————————

Not long ago the City Council of Sacramento, California held a contest to rename the "man-hole" covers in their streets. Apparently, such a designation as "MAN-hole" is blatantly offensive and sexist. Some cities have dealt with this street-level problem by calling them "person-hole" covers. Fortunately, Sacramento was more sensitive about the psyches of their dual-gender work force. After all, the word "person" contains the male designation, "son," so that would never do.

As long as we are on the subject, I wonder why radical feminists allow themselves to be called "women"; it includes the word "men." And "wo-person" isn't a viable option, for again, the chauvinistic term "son" is included. Perhaps "woper" would be acceptable. Anyway, the winning entry in the Sacramento contest was ... drum roll please ... "maintenance hole cover." I'm sure you'll rest easier tonight.

Dear friend, God made men to be men; God made women to be women. The differences between the sexes are declared in God's Word. The differences were programmed in from the beginning, and they are good.

In my opinion, women who seek equality with men lack ambition. My wife has no interest in being my equal. She's not willing to stoop to that level. Adrian Rogers used to say, "Women are infinitely superior to men ... at being women, and men are infinitely superior to women at being men." I couldn't agree more.

When Adam needed a suitable helper, God did not clone Adam. God artfully crafted a wonderful, exotic creature, intentionally made to correspond to man, yet to be different from man.

Consider some of the differences between women and men. I will state generalities, realizing there are exceptions to every rule.

Physical Differences

There are physical differences between men and women. In his book, *Understanding the Man in Your Life*, H. Norman Wright writes:

Men snore more…they fight more…they change their minds more often than women do…their blood is redder…their daylight vision is superior…they have thicker skins and longer vocal chords. Their metabolic rate is higher…more of them are left-handed…they feel pain less than women.…They age earlier but wrinkle later…their immunity against disease is weaker…they talk about themselves less, but worry about themselves more.

Further, a man's skull is almost always thicker and stronger than a woman's. The stereotype of a "thick-headed" man is not far-fetched.

Men tend to be physically stronger than women. But, whereas men are usually stronger in the upper part of their bodies…many women can equal or surpass men in lower body

strength, which comes in handy when babies are born.

Women tend to do better than men in long distance activities like running and swimming. In fact, the first woman to swim the English Channel was Gertrude Ederle, on August 6, 1926.

And she broke the previous men's record time by two hours.[4]

Women tend to live four to eight years longer than men. Someone asked a man, "Why do husbands die before their wives?" He answered, "They want to." But, that simply is not true. A woman's metabolism is slower. It makes it harder for her to lose weight, but also makes her live longer.

Psychological Differences

There are psychological differences as well as physical differences. Women have more efficient access to both sides of their brain. They make greater use of their right brain. Women can focus on more than one problem at one time and frequently prefer to solve problems through multi-tasking.

The right brain, left brain factor affects the way men and women respond to a crisis. Men generally focus on results. Women tend to focus on relationships. When John F. Kennedy was shot, men asked, "Who's in charge of the country? What if Russia attacks right now? How many missiles do we have?" That's left brain logic. In contrast, women responded, "Poor Caroline. Poor John John. Poor Jackie." Right brain caring, and left brain logic are two completely different ways of looking at a crisis. Neither is wrong; they're just different. Both are needed.

A couple sat on the front porch of their country home. It was an idyllic summer evening, right out of a Thomas Kinkade painting. The glow of a big, yellow moon cast soft shadows across the valley. The fragrance of blossoming honeysuckle perfumed the air. A gentle glow illumined the open windows of the country church in the valley below. Choir practice was in session, and the warm breeze transported harmonious praise to where the couple sat in an old swing. Underneath the porch, crickets joined the chorus. She focused on the choir's melody; he thought of collecting the crickets for a morning fishing trip.

"Isn't that beautiful?" she whispered, and leaned her head on his comfortable shoulder.

"Yes, it really is," he said.

"I don't think I've ever heard anything quite as lovely."

"Me either," he said. Then he added, "You know they make that noise by rubbing their hind legs together."

Men and women think differently.

Just as there are physical and psychological differences between men and women, there are also social difference. For most men, the five most frightening words in the English language are, "Let's talk about our relationship."

Men have an extra "Y" chromosome. It causes them to ask, "WHY do we always have to talk about our relationship?"

It isn't that men are indifferent to relationships. They just don't want to talk about them. Wives tend to think, "Our marriage is working as long as we can talk about it." But husbands think, "The relationship isn't working if we have to keep talking about it."

Some things were different about Adam and Eve's marriage, but some things are perpetually the same. The purpose of marriage hasn't changed. Happy, healthy marriages still enjoy deep, intimate, comforting, secure companionship. Further, the need for cooperation between a husband and wife has not changed. A storybook marriage is still a partnership.

Now let's consider...

The Permanence of Marriage: Commitment

God still intends for marriage to last a lifetime. God said, "For this reason a man will leave his father and mother and be united to his wife, and they will become one flesh" (Genesis 2:24 NIV).

The word translated, "united," is a Hebrew word meaning "to weld or glue," as one glues two pieces of paper together. God's plan was and is for one man and one woman to be committed to one another "till death do them part."

The Bible says a man is "united to his wife." He is glued to her; she is glued to him. Have you ever tried to separate two pieces of paper that were glued together? If you do, you damage both pieces. That's why there is no such thing as a painless divorce. There are always casualties.

Unfortunately, many say, "I do," but really don't. At the marriage altar they promise "to love, honor and cherish so long as we both shall live." But in their hearts, they interpret this promise as "so long as we both shall *love*." "Till death do us part," is replaced with, "till disagreement do us part." God, however, intends marriage to be "so long as we both shall live." Permanent commitment is still God's plan for marriage.

God's plan is that 1 + 1 = 1. Adam and Eve became one flesh in marriage, and what God has joined, let no man separate. The Bible says, "The man and his wife were both naked, and they felt no shame" (Genesis 2:25 NIV). What does this last verse of Genesis 2 mean? It means they were so much one that there was no shame, no intimidation; they were willing and able to share everything with one another.

Adam and Eve lived together as man and wife for

centuries. Adam did not die until he was 930 years old. I would call that a lasting relationship, wouldn't you? What are the secrets of a relationship that lasts? Allow me to introduce you to…

The Seven Laws of Longevity
Acceptance

The first law is mutual acceptance. God said, "Accept one another, then, just as Christ accepted you, in order to bring praise to God" (Romans 15:7 NIV). Husbands and wives can accept one another the same way God accepts them—unconditionally.

Dolley Payne Todd, was a new bride at twenty-one. Within three years, she and her husband were the happy parents of two boys. Then, a yellow-fever epidemic swept through their city. All four family members were afflicted, and only two recovered. Dolley's baby and husband died. At twenty-five, she was a widow and the single mom of a two-year-old boy.

Dolley, however, refused to succumb to self-pity and depression. A friend introduced her to a gentleman who was seventeen years her senior. Within a few months, they married. She nicknamed her new husband Jimmy.

Dolley always grabbed center-stage at social functions; everyone knew her as the life of the party. She had blue eyes, fair skin, black curls, and loved to dress in stylish, colorful fashions. Jimmy, on the other hand, took everything seriously. His thoughtful, scholarly approach to life made him a classic introvert. Jimmy was short and plump, and dressed like a mortician going to his own funeral. Two people could have hardly been more different.

Dolley and Jimmy unconditionally accepted one another. Neither tried to change the other, and both benefited. He added gravity to her effervescent personality; she brought a sense of fun to his reserved nature. Because they did not try to change each other, they enjoyed a beautiful, harmonious relationship. She assured Jimmy, "Our hearts understand one another." Mutual acceptance allowed them to complete one another, rather than compete with one another.

You have probably heard of this happy couple, Jimmy and Dolley. They were the fourth president and first lady of the United States—James and Dolley Madison.[v] Their forty-two year marriage thrived on the first law of longevity in relationships: mutual acceptance.

Attention

The second law of longevity in relationships is attention. First Peter 1:22 says, "Love one another deeply from the heart." Easy to say, but how do you do it? What are the actions behind the words, "I love you"?

Complicated? No. It is not as complicated as you might think. May I suggest that another way to spell "love" is A-T-T-E-N-T-I-O-N. Nothing declares "love" as clearly as focusing your attention on a person you accept unconditionally.

Many husbands would be surprised to learn that their wives were desperately yearning for their attention. The husband is always at work, locked away in his workshop, or stretched out down in front of the TV. Nearly every conversation is treated as an interruption... and the wife feels ignored.

In a *Philadelphia Inquirer* article, Stephen Seplow and Jonathan Storm reported that about "40% of all the hours not committed to working, eating, sleeping, or doing chores" are consumed by TV viewing. They noted that by the time the average American dies, he or she has spent a decade in front of a television set!

One wife was fed up. Desperation drove her to a drastic action. She turned the television off during the Super Bowl. In the moment she had her husband's undivided attention, she shouted, "You love football more than you love me." He only made matters worse when he responded, "But honey, I do love you more than baseball."

Dr. John Gottman suggested a simple, practical way for you to transform your marriage by focusing your attention on your spouse... and it only takes five hours a week: THE MAGIC FIVE HOURS. You can follow his marriage transforming formula. It begins with...

Partings. Before you say good-bye in the morning, make sure you have learned one thing happening in your spouse's life that day. It may be as simple as lunch with the boss, a doctor's appointment, or perhaps a scheduled phone call with an old friend. Anything will do, as long as it is important to your spouse.

Time: 2 minutes a day x 5 working days
Total: 10 minutes

Reunions. Be sure to engage in a stress-reducing conversation at the end of each workday. Try not to dump a problem on your spouse the minute he or she walks in the door.
Time: 20 minutes a day x 5 days
Total: 1 hour 40 minutes

Admiration and appreciation. Find some way everyday to communicate genuine affection and appreciation toward your spouse.
Time: 5 minutes a day x 7 days
Total: 35 minutes

Affection: Kiss, hold, and touch each other during the time you're together. Make sure to kiss each other before going to sleep.

Dawn, my wife, affixed a sign directly above the threshold to our master bedroom. It says, ALWAYS KISS ME GOODNIGHT. Take it from me, that is good advice.

Think of that kiss as an opportunity to let go of any minor irritations that have built up over the day. Lace your kiss with forgiveness for and tenderness toward your spouse.
Time: 5 minutes a day x 7 days
Total: 35 minutes

Weekly Date. Ask each other questions … use these dates to talk out a marital issue. If necessary, work through an argument you had that week.

Time: 2 hours once a week
Total: 2 hours
Grand Total: Five hours!

The time required to incorporate these changes into your relationship is minimal. Yet these five hours will help enormously in keeping your marriage on track. First, acceptance. Second, attention. Third...

Adjustment

The third law of longevity in relationships is adjustment. What kind of adjustment? You can adjust to one another's needs, desires, foibles, and idiosyncrasies. The Bible exhorts, "And be subject to one another in the fear of Christ" (Ephesians 5:21 NIV). God calls husbands and wives to mutual submission. If you want a happy marriage, learn to submit to one another.

Someone has said, "When two people get married, it's like a couple of porcupines snuggling up together on a cold winter day. Things are kind of sticky and painful until a few adjustments are made!"

Be willing to change anything about yourself so the marriage can survive. Nothing will kill a marriage like inflexibility and selfishness. Be willing to give as well as take.

Too often, people enter marriage convinced they can change their mate. I have learned a valuable lesson. I cannot adjust Dawn. I cannot change her. I can only change me.

In moments of conflict (yes, pastors have them), sometimes I begin to pray, "Oh, Lord, change my children. Oh,

Lord, change my wife." When I finish my little plea, the answer often comes back: "I intend to, but let's start with your children's father and your wife's husband!" God expects me to make adjustments in the attitudes and actions of the one and only person on the planet I can control.

Acknowledgement

The fourth law of longevity in relationships is acknowledgement. You can acknowledge problems before they become major issues. Don't store things up. Don't sweep disagreements under the rug.

———————————

David and Diane didn't deal with conflict very well. Neither acknowledged the damage David's attitude toward housework was doing to their marriage. David ignored the simple things he could do to keep their home tidy. Diane said nothing, but thought, "If he really cared, he would know how I feel." Her anger quietly grew.

One day David arrived home to the sound of hammering in their bedroom. He walked in to find Diane, still in her business suit, nailing his dirty boxer shorts to the oak floor.

"They've been here for three days," Diane fumed. "I figured you wanted them to be a permanent part of the décor."

———————————

I doubt that helped the décor or the marriage, but I bet it got his *attention*. Both needed to *acknowledge* a problem. He had failed to make *adjustments* to something that was

extremely important to his wife. She failed to give unconditional *acceptance* to her sloppy husband. Their evening
began with stress-escalating confrontation, rather than
stress-reducing conversation.

➤ It's hard to be gentle when you are bursting with bitterness. If your heart rate exceeds 100 beats per minute,
you won't hear what your spouse tells you, no matter how
hard you try. So don't wait too long before bringing up
an issue—otherwise it will escalate in your mind. As the
Bible says, "Let not the sun go down upon your wrath"
(Ephesians 4:26 NIV).

Amnesty

The fifth law of longevity in relationships is amnesty.
Love forgives offences, and Jesus Christ is our ultimate
example. "Be kind to one another, tender-hearted, forgiving each other, just as God in Christ also has forgiven
you" (Ephesians 4:32 NIV).

Much-loved grandparents celebrated their fiftieth wedding anniversary. Their daughter asked, "Mama, what is
the key to the happiness and joy you and Daddy have
known through the years? Tell us your secret."

"Well," she began, "the night before your daddy and
I were married, I thought of a list of ten things I would
overlook about his personality—things I didn't like. The
day we walked down the aisle, I made a promise that when

any of those ten things came up, I would overlook it for the sake of marital harmony."

"Granny," one of her granddaughters excitedly replied, "please tell us that list. Tell us the ten things!"

"Honey," she answered, "to be honest, I never did write them down. But every time your grandfather did something to make me hopping mad, I would think, 'Lucky for him it's one of those ten things.'"

Learn to forgive. In fact, the Bible teaches to forgive your mate 490 times and more (Matt. 18:21–22 NIV).

Appreciation

The sixth law of longevity in relationships is appreciation. "Therefore encourage one another and build each other up, just as in fact you are doing" (1 Thessalonians. 5:11 NIV).

Many people think the secret to reconnecting with their partner is a candlelight dinner or a by-the-sea vacation. However, the real secret is to show each other your appreciation in little ways every day. A romantic night out only turns up the heat when a couple has kept the pilot light burning by showing appreciation in other ways. Show your appreciation with:

- A surprise gift. It doesn't have to cost much, but it will pay big dividends.

- A quick phone call or text message that says, "Thank you for mating my socks. You're beautiful."

- Sending flowers to your wife's mother saying, "Thanks for raising such a wonderful daughter."

When you show appreciation, you store up goodwill. It will serve as a cushion when times inevitably get rough. During those tough times, your spouse will be able to make allowances for you.

I also recommend strategically "spreading good reports" about your husband or wife. When you say good things to a friend or relative, your words of affirmation will likely make it back to your spouse's ears. Your mate will know what an important place he or she has in your heart. Finally...

Affection

The seventh law of longevity in relationships is affection. First Peter 3:8 NIV says, "Live in harmony with one another; be sympathetic, love as brothers, be compassionate and humble."

Marriage is friendship that catches fire. Showing affection will keep that blaze burning.

Years ago, children collected Coke bottles to return to the grocery store for money. A nickel deposit had been paid when the Coke was purchased, so one received a nickel for each bottle returned. Then there came a bottle with a strange slogan: No deposit, no return! If you put nothing in, you get nothing back!

The same will hold true in all of life—your marriage, your children, your job, and your relationship with God. No deposit, no return.

The Bible often speaks of God's love for you and me.

We are valuable to Him. He delights in us. He proved His affection when He sent Jesus Christ to die for us.

Are you honoring or breaking the seven laws of longevity in relationships? Do you and your spouse give to one another acceptance, attention, adjustment, acknowledgement, amnesty, appreciation, and affection? If you regularly make deposits, long-term returns are guaranteed.

Conclusion

Bob and Sarah had a storybook marriage that lasted sixty years plus. They understood that the purpose of marriage is companionship. They were so much in love—they touched, laughed, teased, and played. Their partnership exemplified cooperation. Their commitment was permanent.

From the early days of their union, they played a crazy game no one else understood. They wrote a funny little word on a piece of paper and hid it in different places around the house. The word was "SHMILY."

Sometimes Sarah looked in the sugar bowl, and there it was: SHMILY. Bob would get out of the shower and see it written across the steamed up mirror: SHMILY. Once Sarah unrolled a whole roll of toilet paper and wrote it on the last sheet: SHMILY.

They played this game their entire married life. Their children knew about the game, but did not know what SHMILY meant. They weren't even sure of how to pronounce it.

Not long after Bob and Sarah's fifty-second wedding anniversary, doctors diagnosed Sarah with cancer. She battled the disease for nearly ten years. Everyone marveled as they watched this couple stand together through it all. And all the while they continued their SHMILY game. Then, one day, Sarah died.

The funeral provided a sad, but glorious time of celebrating Sarah's wonderful life. The children, the grandchildren, and by now even great-grandchildren watched Bob as he said good-bye to his beloved wife, his teammate for more than sixty years.

Silence reigned on the drive to the cemetery. When they arrived at the graveside, they all noticed the big pink ribbon on the casket—and there it was, in big letters on the ribbon: SHMILY! They watched as Bob approached the casket and in a soft, deep voice began to sing to her. As one, the family held hands and began to cry. It was a bittersweet moment.

As the graveside service concluded, most everyone quietly moved away so Bob could have a moment alone. One granddaughter, a young teenager, stayed behind. She reached out and held his hand, comforting herself as much as him.

"Grandpa," she said, "tell me, what SHMILY means?"

Bob looked into her eyes. With a tender smile he replied, "SHMILY stands for 'See How Much I Love You.'"

And yes, everyone could see. Like Adam and Eve, Bob and Sarah personified the purpose, the partnership, and the permanence of marriage. How about your marriage? Is it growing according to God's original plan? Is it becoming *a storybook marriage*?

Dumbo
The Five Foolish Mistakes of Marriage

Approximately a year of preparation is necessary for a sixteen-year-old to earn a Driver's License in my state. Shortly before the fifteenth birthday, future licensees typically obtain a *Driver's Handbook*. This driving encyclopedia is diligently studied to gain the knowledge required to pass a written exam. Only after passing an exhaustive exam can a young person have a learner's permit. Then a driver's education course follows with many hours of practice driving with a parent or guardian. Before the actual road test, the state requires each student driver to complete a four-hour, online "Drug Alcohol Traffic Awareness" course. By the time the Driver's License is earned, a sixteen-year-old can look back on many hours of preparation over twelve–plus months. Only after running this gauntlet is a new driver turned loose on the freeways as financial fodder for every radar gun in the state.

Consider the science of cosmetology. Formal training, a state exam and license is required to give a crew cut or trim somebody's toenails. Likewise, training and a license are required to give a massage.

But here's the irony. To get a marriage license that empowers you to create new life, destroy your life, and crush the dreams and hopes of your spouse and family, all you have to do is have $61 dollars and a pulse. It's absolutely amazing to me … no, actually, it's unbelievable. Despite all of the societal damage inflicted by divorce, some states may give any human being with brains enough to find the front door of the courthouse a license to marry.

Is it any wonder that the chance of a first marriage ending in divorce after forty years is sixty-seven percent? In fact, half of all divorces occur in the first seven years, and the divorce rate for second marriages is as much as ten percent higher than for first-timers.

I believe, without question, the number one social problem in our country today is divorce. When a home flies apart at the seams, it scars the couple, the children, the in-laws, the grandparents, the friends, and even the church. Indeed, you'd be hard-pressed to name one of society's ills that cannot be traced directly or indirectly to the breakdown of the family. Is it any wonder that God hates divorce (Malachi 2:16 NIV)? Notice, I did not say God hates divorced people.

Don't misunderstand. I'm not calling for the state or federal government to mandate marriage instruction. We can only imagine the fiasco that would become. I am, however, suggesting the Bible is God's instruction manual for marriage; Bible-believing churches and Christian homes must take the lead in preparing couples for marriage.

Because many couples have had no instruction, they sabotage their own relationships. They make foolish mistakes. In fact, I have repeatedly observed five foolish mistakes couples make. Hence, the title of this chapter, "Dumbo."

In this chapter, we discover God's marriage manual. These principles are found in the New Testament book of Ephesians. When he wrote Ephesians, the apostle Paul was imprisoned in Rome. Paul had spent over three years in the great metropolitan city of Ephesus. There he had planted a dynamic church. The believers were precious to him. Many of them were his spiritual children and he was their spiritual father. A few years had passed since Paul had been in their presence, yet he had heard of some of their needs. So he wrote an inspired letter to give special instructions about how a church family should function. In light of what we have been learning about the priority God places on marriage, we aren't surprised to find that significant instructions for happy, functional families are included in God's directives for the local church.

Human nature guarantees we will all make mistakes in life and in marriage. There have been no perfect marriages since Genesis 2, because there have been no perfect people since Genesis 3. But there is hope. God forgives sin and redeems sinners through Jesus Christ (Ephesians 2). That's good news. Forgiven and redeemed people are empowered and eternally transformed. We can learn to avoid the foolish mistakes that sabotage our marriages. Paul said, "Therefore do not be foolish, but understand what the Lord's will is" (Eph. 5:17 NIV).

I'm told that there were two fellows who went to the theater to enjoy a western film. At the climactic scene, one turned to the other and whispered, "I'll bet you fifty bucks the cowboy rides his horse under that tree, and a tree branch knocks him plumb out of the saddle." The other said, "You're on." A moment later, sure enough, the cowpoke rode under the tree and the branch knocked him right out of the saddle. Rather than gloat, the first man began to feel guilty. He confessed to his friend, "I can't take your money. I saw this film yesterday. I knew what was going to happen." The second man said, "That's okay. I saw it too. But I didn't think the guy would make the same mistake twice!"

The Apostle Paul is trying to help his people stop being foolish by repeating mistakes. In fact, in Ephesians 5:17 NIV, Paul uses two contrasting words: "foolish" and "understand." Foolishness follows a lack of understanding. And many couples repeatedly make five foolish mistakes because they lack understanding. These are DUMBO errors. So let's use the word DUMBO as an acrostic to see if you are making any of these.

First, one of the most foolish mistakes married people make is...

Delaying to Cut the Apron Strings

I see this principle in Ephesians 5:31 NIV, "For this reason a man will leave his father and mother and be united to his wife, and the two will become one flesh." The commandment appears in the Bible *four times*.[1]

Whatever God commands is important. Once is enough. When He commands something twice, we should put a star by it or underline it. But four times! Do you get the idea He's trying to get our full attention? When God considers something significant enough to repeat it four times, we can be certain it's vitally important!

Perhaps you remember this verse from the previous chapter. Paul quoted Genesis 2:24. Right at the beginning of Adam and Eve's relationship as husband and wife, God commanded that the biblical pattern was to leave father and mother and be united to one another. Obviously this was a command for future generations, not for Adam and Eve. They had no parents to leave. But they soon had children they were to release to form their own families. So, as Paul discusses marriage, he quotes the command.

The most famous version of Genesis 2:24 is in the *King James Version* of the Bible. You're probably familiar with it: "Therefore shall a man leave his father and his mother, and shall cleave unto his wife: and they shall be one flesh."

Marriage is a two-step dance. *Leaving* is the first step. You leave Mommy and Daddy. You are no longer under their roof or authority. *Cleaving* is the second step. You set up a new home and go out on your own.

When a man and woman "leave" and "cleave" they become "one." They become one physically, emotionally, and mentally. I call this "God's divine math": 1 + 1 = 1. A husband and wife are one flesh, they share one agenda, and they look forward to one future.

For this reason, I won't marry a couple unless the man is capable of supporting his family. If they're dead broke, the new couple inevitably winds up in Mommy and Daddy's home … and they make a foolish mistake. They delay cutting the apron strings.

The uncut apron strings are the source of most mother-in-law jokes. Mothers-in-law aren't evil. It just seems that way when one has to compete with her for a spouse's love, loyalty, and attention. Mother-in-law jokes are funny only because they contain kernels of truth. Also, many people use humor to deal with pain.

My all-time favorite mother-in-law joke opens with a man leaving a *7–11* with his morning coffee. He notices a most unusual funeral procession approaching the nearby cemetery. Two long black hearses, about fifty feet apart, lead the procession. Behind the second hearse is a solitary man walking a pit bull on a leash. Some 200 men, walking in single file, follow them.

The man at the *7–11* is overcome by curiosity. He respectfully approaches the man walking the dog and says, "I'm so sorry for your loss. I realize this is a bad time to disturb you, but I've never seen a funeral like this. Whose funeral is it?"

The man replies, "My wife is in the first hearse."

"What happened to her?"

"My dog attacked and killed her."

"I'm very sorry," the first man says. Then he asks, "And who is in the second hearse?"

"My mother-in-law," the man answers. "She was trying to save her daughter when the dog turned on her."

A poignant and thoughtful moment of silence passes between the two men. Finally the first man asks, "Could I borrow that dog?"

"Get in line."

You don't hear father-in-law jokes. Why? Because at the core of the tension is a turf battle between two women vying for one man's love. A very intimate bond exists between a boy and his mother. She has nurtured him … cared for him … sacrificed for him all of his growing-up years. Marriage inserts a new woman into the mother's place in the young man's life, and she feels sidelined. If the apron stings are not cut, inevitably, there will be friction.

One writer tells about the crisis David and Janie faced when his parents came for a weekend visit to the newlywed's home. Janie had made Saturday dinner reservations for the couples at their favorite Italian restaurant. She was excited about showing the restaurant off to her Italian in-laws. The dinner reservations were especially important to her because she often felt upstaged by her mother-in-law who was very knowledgeable about Italian cuisine.

On Saturday afternoon, while Janie and David were out running errands, the mother-in-law went to the butcher and the supermarket. She then prepared David's favorite dish for dinner—osso bucco.

When David and Janie arrived home, the savory aroma of garlic and veal wafted through the air. Janie was furious—but not surprised—when David's mother said she "forgot" about the reservations. David was face-to-face with a dilemma. The veal looked delicious, and he knew how hurt his mother would be if he didn't eat it. He really wanted to tell Janie to cancel the reservations.

Although this hardly sounds like a major crisis, it was a turning point in David and Janie's marriage. Janie held her breath as she watched David survey the feast his mother had prepared. He cleared his throat, put his arm around his mother, and thanked her for cooking such a wonderful meal. Then he insisted it would keep for another day in the refrigerator. He explained, "It's very important to me and to Janie that you allow us to share our favorite Saturday night retreat with you and Dad."

His mother was highly offended. She got teary-eyed and made a bit of a scene. (David let his father deal with that.) But it was worth it for David to see Janie's look of joy and triumph. In the end, David's message was loud and clear: "Janie comes first, Mom. Get used to it."

The only way out of such a dilemma is for the husband to side with his wife against his mother. "Our real marriage began," Janie recalls, "when he let his mother know that I was now first in his heart."

When you get married, two primary apron strings must be cut. First, there's the ...

Counseling String

As our children grow up, they need our advice. They need our wisdom. And it feels good being needed. But after children marry, we need to back off and let our married children work out their own problems.

When I do pre-marital counseling, during the last session before the wedding ceremony, I actually sit down with the parents and explain their new role to them. They are no longer to offer advice—ever—unless they are asked. They are to bite their tongues, even to the point of gnawing them off.

Likewise, I tell young couples that when conflicts or issues inevitably arise, they are forbidden to call Mom and Dad. "It's your problem. Work it out." Meanwhile, I tell the parents, "If they call you ... tell them to go home and work it out."

Why? Because you are to *leave* and to *cleave*. And when leaving and cleaving is done properly, you can have a wonderful relationship with your in-laws.

Consider Naomi, the consummate mother-in-law. She had a beautiful relationship with her daughter-in-law, Ruth (Ruth 1:6–22 NIV). Think about Jethro, the father-in-law of Moses. Jethro was enormously supportive of Moses, and actually helped him devise a plan to keep from working himself to death (Exodus 18). In-law relations do not have to be toxic.

Second, you must cut the ...

Economic String

Some married couples stay too closely attached to parents and in-laws because of money.

Parents, I know you're only trying to help. You have pure, altruistic motives ... and you're only giving help out of love. But what you're really doing is creating dependence ... and you're going to create resentment, too. I guarantee it.

Whether you recognize it or not, your gifts always come with strings attached. Just watch. The first time the young couple makes a decision that you question, you'll hear yourself saying, *"After all I've done for you, you're going to do that?!"*

When your married children became heavily dependent on you financially, you won't be able to help yourself—you're going to manipulate them. You'll expect them to be at your home every Christmas. You'll expect them to abide by your wishes. And not surprisingly, they will become extremely bitter.

That's why I'm now repeating for the third time man must be financially capable of supporting his family before I will marry them. One of the things I'm trying to prevent is a train wreck with in-laws.

The first Dumbo mistake young married couples make is delaying to cut the apron strings. God was serious when He repeatedly commanded, "For this reason a man will leave his father and mother and be united to his wife, and the two will become one flesh" (Ephesians 5:31).

The second dumbo mistake is ...

Underestimating the Power of Temptation

> God warned through the apostle Paul, "But among you there must not be even a hint of sexual immorality, ... Let no one deceive you with empty words, for because of such things God's wrath comes on those who are disobedient. Therefore do not be partners with them."
>
> Ephesians 5:3, 6–7 (NIV)

Sexual immorality is dangerous and damaging. There are people in the world who will try to deceive you with their cunning, seductive words. Paul says, "Do not be partners with them." Don't join them in their practices; don't support their causes.

Temptations abound. Erotica flows into our homes from America's television networks; suggestive billboards line the highways; pornography is in sports magazines; internet chat rooms are readily available on your office computer. A women's magazine surveyed a group of men. They asked, "Which marriage vow is the hardest to keep?"

Some of the responses were:

- To love "in sickness and in health"—19%
- To love "for richer or for poorer"—19%
- "Forsaking all others"—60%

Why would men say the toughest of all wedding vows is "forsaking all others"? Because there's so much temptation, and I don't think you ever outgrow it. I asked a friend of mine ... ninety-two years old ... how old do you have to be before pretty girls are no longer a temptation. He dryly said, "I don't know."

So, is it hopeless? Are we the powerless victims of temptation? No, it is not hopeless. God does not ask us to do what cannot be done. You can overcome temptation.

Overcoming Temptation

I have found seven principles for overcoming temptation helpful in my own life. I believe they will help you as well. By the way, men aren't the only ones vulnerable to temptation.

Realize Your Vulnerability

"The heart is deceitful above all things and beyond cure. Who can understand it?" (Jeremiah 17:9). Be especially guarded when you are at an emotional or physical low point. When you are feeling discouraged, needy, lonely, abandoned, and dejected, it is easy to reach for something, or someone, to fill that emptiness or relieve that pain. Realize your vulnerability.

Remain on Guard

Temptation rarely comes to us as an obvious assault, but usually as a sly subterfuge, a deceptive ploy. Remember, "Satan himself transforms himself into an angel of light" (2 Corinthians 11:14). Never reward yourself with the titillation of temptation. Remain on guard. You may be more vulnerable at one time than another, but you are always vulnerable, especially if you toy with temptation. Therefore...

Run From Tempting Situations

It's been my experience that women flee from temptation while men crawl away with the fond hope it will overtake them. But the Bible says clearly, "Flee from sexual immorality. All other sins a man commits are outside his body, but he who sins sexually sins against his own body" (1 Corinthians 6:18 NIV).

Said another way, "If you don't want to eat the devil's apples, stay out of his orchard."

Sometimes we say, "There is safety in *numbers*." That's true. But there's more safety in *exodus*! Get out of there! Get out of those places or situations where you might fall. Don't play chicken to see how close you can get to the edge of the cliff of sin without falling over. No! Flee sexual immorality. Hold each other accountable by regular, open discussions.

Request God's Help

God said, "Call upon me in the day of trouble; I will deliver you" (Psalm 50:15 NIV). When you are tempted, close your eyes and talk with God. Ask Him to deliver you. His promise, "I will deliver you," is true. Isn't that good news? Trust Him.

Refocus Your Attention

Your mind is only capable of tuning in one station at a time. You can only think one thought at a time. Whenever you're tempted, change the channel of your mind. That's why Paul didn't waste time telling you what NOT to think about. Instead he said, "Finally, brothers, whatever is true, whatever is noble, whatever is right, whatever is pure, whatever is lovely, whatever is admirable—if anything is excellent or praiseworthy—think about such things" (Philippians 4:8 NIV).

Reveal Your Struggle

"Two are better than one, because they have a good return for their work: If one falls down, his friend can help him up. But pity the man who falls and has no one to help him up!" (Ecclesiastes 4:9–10). At the church I pastor, we have "Celebrate Recovery" groups. These are great places for people to meet other believers who are struggling with the same kinds of temptations. People work together. They help one another up when they fall, and they help one another keep from falling.

Don't let pride stand in the way of your victory over temptation. Admit that you need help and cannot make it on your own. Accept the responsibility of finding a godly friend or support group to help you.

Resist the Devil

Don't give up without a fight. "Resist the devil, and he will flee from you" (James 4:7 NIV). Sound impossible? It's not. You can resist the devil.

Two steps may be helpful. Step one: *determine in advance what you will do when temptation comes*. It's hard to make right choices when you're under pressure . . . so having a battle plan is smart. The best defense is a good offense. Step two: *recite scripture*. If you study and memorize Bible verses, you will be armed in advance against the enemy of your integrity. If this strategy was good for our Lord Jesus, it will be good for you (Matthew 4:1–11 NIV).

The next foolish mistake in our DUMBO acronym is the letter M...

Manipulating with Money, Sex, or Silence

A man has needs; a woman has needs. Everyone has needs, and that is good. God made us this way. Marriage, however, is a relationship in which my needs must be subservient to my wife's needs. And from her perspective, my needs must take precedence over her own. The Bible explains:

> Submit to one another out of reverence for Christ. Wives, submit to your husbands as to the Lord. For the husband is the head of the wife as Christ is the head of the church, his body, of which he is the Savior. Now as the church submits to Christ, so also wives should submit to their husbands in everything.
>
> Ephesians 5:21–23 (NIV)

The whole issue of submission is a super-charged subject in our politically correct world. So called "evangelical feminists" have latched on to Ephesians 5:21 as a means of saying, "See, we are to be *mutually* submissive. Husbands must submit to wives just as much as wives must submit to their husbands.

True, the Bible does speak of mutual submission.

But verse 21 does not nullify verse 22, and they are not in contradiction.

God established a hierarchy in the home. The man of the house is never to be a tyrant or dictator. But the man is to lead. He is to be a servant leader, like Jesus. The husband submits to the heavenly Father and the wife submits to the husband.

Submission is not a matter of inferiority. It is a matter of order, hierarchy, and leadership. Proper submission celebrates unity and engenders harmony. Jesus Christ is the greatest example of this fact.

Jesus Christ is God in human flesh. He is the Second Person of the triune Godhead. He is not inferior to either God the Father or God the Holy Spirit. The three Persons of the Godhead are co-equal and co-eternal. Yet, Jesus Christ submits to the Father. During His earthly sojourn He declared, "For I have come down from heaven not to do my will but to do the will of him who sent me" (John 6:38 NIV). There is no conflict in the Godhead; there is not inferiority, but there is order and hierarchy.

Further, Jesus Christ honored the order in the home. He, the creator of the world, submitted to His earthly parents. "Then he went down to Nazareth with them and was obedient to them. But his mother treasured all these things in her heart" (Luke 2:51 NIV). Certainly Jesus was not inferior to Joseph and Mary. He was their Creator (John 1:1–3 NIV) and their Savior (Luke 2:46–47 NIV). Yet He willingly submitted to their leadership. He respected and celebrated the order and harmony of the home.

A marriage is in trouble when both parties start looking

out for #1. Rather than preferring the needs of your spouse over your own, you start manipulating. Unfortunately, I regularly meet manipulating couples. Their whole marriage is a vicious cycle of manipulation and bargaining.

- He says, "I'll buy that pretty new dress for you if you'll do what I want."

- She says, "I'll make tonight unforgettable for you if you'll do what I want."

- He says, "I'll take you on that dream vacation if you'll do what I want."

And when they don't get their way, on comes the silent treatment.

"What's wrong?"

"Nothing!"

"Don't tell me that! I know something's wrong. What is it?"

"If you loved me—*you'd know*."

All of that is a manipulation. It's ungodly! It's demonic! It will drive a dagger into the heart of your marriage. My friend, unless you're a dumbo, you'll stop manipulating today!

The next foolish mistake to avoid starts with "B"…

Being Reckless with Words

Some couples use their tongues to *blast* instead of *bless*. Washington Irving was correct when, in *Rip Van Winkle*, he observed, "The tongue is the only tool that grows sharper with constant use."

I once heard the argument through the paper-thin walls of a hotel. I had no interest in eavesdropping on the couple next door, but I had no choice. It started as a mild disagreement. It soon escalated into a hostile confrontation. Before it was through, war was underway. The couple screamed at one another at the top of their lungs ... calling each other names. Trust me, "honey" and "sweetheart" weren't on the list. Before long, the door slammed and one of them walked out. While I was glad for the ceasefire, I knew they were just regrouping to re-engage the battle another day. Could that have been you and your spouse in the next room?

The Bible places a high value on wholesome speech. For example, let's walk quickly through Ephesians 4:25–32 NIV. A Christian husband and wife can and should speak to one another with far different attitudes than are prevalent among unbelievers (compare Ephesians 4:17–24 NIV). You can abandon the old habits of reckless words and begin to use wise, loving words. How? Follow these six principles.

Never Deceive

First, never try to deceive your spouse. Instead, "each of you must put off falsehood and speak truthfully to his neighbor [Isn't your spouse your closest neighbor?], for we are all members of one body" (Eph. 4:25 NIV). If both of you have received Jesus Christ as your Lord and Savior, both of you are parts of the body of Christ. Also, marriage made you "one flesh" (Genesis 2:24 NIV). Deceiving your spouse is deceiving yourself. That's one reason the Bible says to "put off falsehood and speak truthfully."

Nothing is more damaging to a relationship than deception. You may tell the truth 999 times a day … but if you tell one lie … that will be the most memorable thing you said. And your spouse will likely suspect the 999 true statements.

Never Speak in Anger

That's usually when you say things you later regret. Ephesians 4 continues, "In your anger do not sin" (v. 26).

When you speak or act inappropriately, do you say, "That really wasn't me; I admit I have a temper, but that wasn't the real me"? I have news for you: that was and is the real you. How you respond to a conflict reveals the real person inside.

What happens when you put a tea bag in a cup of hot water? The water soon turns brown. Why? Did the hot water turn itself brown? No. The "brownness" was in the tea bag the whole time; the hot water merely brought out its natural color.

What happens when you squeeze a lemon? Sour juice emerges. Did the squeezing make the lemon sour? No. The squeezing merely brought out the natural sourness.

In the same way, when you find yourself in "hot water" or "being squeezed" by your marriage, what comes out is what's inside. Stress and conflict unmask the real you.

Most married people would be wise to pray with the psalmist, "Set a guard over my mouth, O Lord; keep watch over the door of my lips" (Psalm 141:3 NIV). The Lord will help you avoid saying the wrong thing at the wrong time. He will also help you say the right thing at the right time. A good dose of gentle, kind words will settle many conflicts. "A gentle answer turns away wrath, but a harsh word stirs up anger" (Proverbs 15:1 NIV). So pick your words carefully.

Never Hold a Grudge

In marriage, there will always be disagreements. That's okay. As I said in Chapter 2, if you agree about everything, one of you isn't necessary. Disagreements can help your relationship, your family, your finances, and your future. So don't get angry when your partner disagrees. Listen to the reasons. Discuss them openly. Both of you may learn. But don't sabotage the whole process by getting angry and holding a grudge. Ephesians 4 goes on to say, "[26]Do not let the sun go down while you are still angry, [27]and do not give the devil a foothold."

Learn from your disagreements. Talk through your differences, and do it today. Don't leave your anger to sit, soak and sour overnight. If you do, you give the devil a foothold in your marriage. Anger should never be your last emotion as you drift off to sleep. Dawn and I accomplish this by "touching toes." We do it gently. We don't kick one another. When we have a disagreement and can't come to a consensus, we finally reach the point where we'll just touch toes in bed. That's our way of saying, "I love you and I know we're going to work this out."

Never Personalize a Problem

Some couples react to disagreements by insulting their spouse with nasty names. Calling your spouse spiteful epithets hurts rather than heals. It declares your spouse to be the problem rather than the problem being the problem. Never focus the argument on your spouse. Instead, work on the problem. Notice Ephesians 4, "[29]Do not let any unwholesome talk come out of your mouths, but only what is helpful for building others up according to their needs, that it may benefit those who listen."

Personalizing a problem escalates disagreements. It is "unwholesome" as well as unholy. It isn't "helpful." It tears down, rather than "building up." It doesn't "benefit" your spouse, nor does it solve the problem.

Never Fight Dirty

I can't explain it more clearly than the apostle Paul. He urged, "[31]Get rid of all bitterness, rage and anger, brawling and slander, along with every form of malice." Life is too short to be bitter.

Never Forget to Forgive

The Bible says, "Be kind and compassionate to one another, forgiving each other, just as in Christ God forgave you."

Jesus Christ has forgiven so much in your life ... doesn't it behoove you to do the same for your spouse? When the dust settles, if you obey this command, you'll still be together.

Deception, anger, grudges, personalizing problems, fighting dirty, and refusing to forgive are all reckless words and attitudes. Being reckless with words is one of the *Dumbo* mistakes in marriage. Why would you torpedo your marriage with reckless words? Did you forget that you are in the boat, too?

A woman's letter expressed her desperate search for hope. She began with a story. When she and her husband were newlyweds, they moved into a small apartment. Soon they heard a noise in the ceiling and discovered a mouse was sharing their apartment, but not contributing to the rent. The woman could tolerate many things, but mice were not on the list.

Her energetic new husband went to work. He set out baited traps, and they waited for the inevitable. Sure enough, in a day or two, they caught the unwanted "roommate." Unfortunately, the mousetrap did not kill it. Now they had an ethical problem; they didn't want to, or maybe they were afraid to kill it in cold blood. What were they to do?

Her letter went on to describe how they placed the mouse, trap and all, in a bucket of water. They thought the cleanest, quickest, and most compassionate way to dispatch the little creature would be to drown it.

They were willing to do the deed, but didn't want to watch the struggle. So, they dunked the mouse, put the bucket out of the way, and left the house for a while.

When they returned, they were shocked to discover that the mouse was still struggling to stay alive. It had managed to prop itself up on the trap and keep its tiny nose just above the water line.

Her letter did not say what happened to the mouse. That wasn't her concern. Instead, she said, "My marriage has been like that mouse for years—standing on one aching toe with its nose just barely out of the water."

She desperately needed help and hope. Is that where you are? If so, it may be because you've made the biggest mistake of all...

Operating Without Jesus in Control

WE FEAR FAIL WHEN WE TRY TO DO IT OURSELVES

I wish you and your spouse, and Dawn and I were together at my favorite coffee shop right now. I would like to lean across the table and talk to both of you up close and personal. I wish you could see in my eyes just how serious I am about this mistake.

The fifth, and biggest, *Dumbo* mistake is trying to manage your marriage without Jesus Christ being in control of your life and home. Please don't read this as pious religious rhetoric. It's far more serious and personal. Operating without Jesus in control virtually guarantees misery is in your future. This is the single most important mistake and I won't perform the wedding of a couple who is making it.

On the other hand, if you will abandon this mistake and receive Jesus into your life and marriage I can guarantee you the power to manage the other four. You'll be able to cut the apron strings and overcome temptation. You'll no longer feel the need for manipulation and reckless words.

Jesus Christ is Lord. If you would master your marriage, you must first let Christ master you. Listen again to the apostle Paul's inspired words. "²²You were taught, with regard to your former way of life, to put off your old self, which is being corrupted by its deceitful desires; ²³to be made new in the attitude of your minds; ²⁴and to put on the new self, created to be like God in true righteousness and holiness" (Ephesians 4:22–24 NIV).

Have you been wishing for a new spouse? Here's how you can have one and how you *can be one*. By faith, both of you can "put off your old self." And why wouldn't you want to? After all, "your old self, … is being corrupted by its deceitful desires." Would your marriage be different if both of you were "made new in the attitude of your minds"? Of course it would. You would be delivered from these *Dumbo* mistakes.

You can abandon your "old self," and "put on the new self, created to be like God in true righteousness and holiness." You can move from a "corrupted" self to a "created" self. You will no longer be controlled by "deceitful desires"; you will be "like God," functioning as God created you to be. You do that by becoming a fully-devoted follower of Jesus Christ.

I've already said that divorce is a national epidemic. A national magazine noted that in so-called God-blessed America, marriages are in crisis. Many quickly add, "And the statistics are no different for Christians than for non-Christians." But I'm happy to tell you, that simply isn't true.

According to the magazine article, of the surveyed marriages that began with a church wedding, only one out of fifty ended in divorce. However, where both husband and wife were married in a church, attend regularly, and have some kind of family devotions, only 1 in 1005 end in divorce. So when all else fails, let's go back and read the instructions.

Why does being a Christian have such a powerful impact on marriage? Allow me to illustrate.

Suppose a couple decides to build a house. They purchase property. Then the wife hires an architect, a contractor, and, for good measure, an interior decorator. The husband likewise hires an architect, contractor, and decorator. Everyone shows up at the same time, on the same lot—ready to build the house. One contractor starts on the west side of the lot with plans drawn by the husband's architect. His crew begins building a single level, ranch-style house. At the same time, on the east side of the lot, the other contractor starts building a two-story, Victorian style house. Would you anticipate any problems during construction?

A few compromises might be possible. If she wants yellow paint and he likes blue, they might agree to compromise with green. But would they ever get a wall up to paint? Wouldn't it be a lot better if they started with the same architect, contractor, and decorator? Can you imagine the advantages of having a single set of plans?

You and your mate are not trying to build a house. You are building something far more important. You are building a home that God can bless.

God is the designer of marriage. God builds the home. If you want your marriage to truly succeed, invite Jesus

Christ to be the head of your life and your home. Here's how. Take your spouse's hand and pray together:

> *Dear God, we realize that our marriage can never be all that you intend until we are both surrendered to Your will. So right now, we each give our lives to You, holding nothing back. We admit that we are sinners. We believe that Jesus Christ died for our sins on the cross and rose again on the third day. From this day forward, we will follow Him as Lord. We will unite our lives with a Bible-believing church. Thank You for saving us. In Jesus name we pray, Amen.*

Forrest Pollock

Bed Knobs and Bored Stiff

Revelation 2:1–7

Do you remember when your love was brand new? Do you remember those first days of being in love and getting engaged? I do, just like it was yesterday.

After being screened by Dawn's parents after that concert years ago to make sure I was a church member and not an ax murderer, they consented and Dawn agreed to go out with me. Man, I was excited!

I could hardly wait to get to her house. "Love is patient" (1 Cor. 13:4a NIV); but boy was I impatient *to be with* her! Also, "love is kind . . . it keeps no record of wrongs" (v. 4b, 5d). Obviously, the Oklahoma City Police were not in love. They were not kind. They did keep records of wrongs. They gave me two speeding tickets the first month Dawn and I dated.

I loved Dawn from the moment I saw her. I wanted

to know everything about her. On our first date, I learned that she loved *Oreo* cookies … so I took Oreos on our second date. And then I proposed.

It's easy for me to preach on heaven. It's familiar territory. I have been there since the moment Dawn said yes. Even today, eighteen years and six children later, my wife is still …

- The doublestuff in my *Oreo* …
- The salt on my french fries …
- The syrup on my pancakes …
- The sizzle on my steak …
- The cream in my coffee …
- The cherry on my sundae …
- The frosting on my cake …

Honestly, I love that girl more today than I did on our wedding day.

I realize, however, that not all married people maintain "that lovin' feelin'" for their spouses. Their relationships sink rather than soar. For example, I heard about a couple who had been married for fifty years. "Things have really changed," the wife said. "You used to sit close to me."

"Well, I can remedy that," her husband replied. He moved next to her on the couch.

"And you used to hold me tight."

"How's that?" he asked as he held her close.

"Do you remember how you used to nuzzle my neck and nibble on my ear lobes?"

He jumped to his feet to leave the room.

"Where are you going?" she shouted.

"I'll be right back," he said. "I've got to get my teeth!"

What is it that drains an erstwhile happy marriage of its spontaneity and excitement? What makes Barbara Streisand sing to Neil Diamond, *"You don't bring me flowers anymore"*?

How about the romance in *your* marriage? How would you describe it? Is it flourishing or floundering?

This chapter is about romance in marriage. I'll confess; it's one of my favorite subjects. And I want to draw your attention to an unlikely portion of Scripture to illustrate how to rekindle romance: Revelation 2.

Revelation

The mention of the book of Revelation in this context may shock some. Perhaps you're thinking, "What does Revelation have to say about romance? Isn't that a book about the end of the world?" Well, hang on. I think you're going to be pleasantly surprised.

Romance Writer?

John, the beloved apostle, isn't usually listed among the great romantic writers. You won't see a list of best-selling Romance authors:

#3 Nora Roberts
#2 Beverly Lewis
#1 The Apostle John

But I propose that his romance writing is of the highest order. And it is the real stuff, not fictional fluff.

John wrote the book of Revelation near the end of the first century a.d. The Roman Emperor, Domitian, who was notorious for his hatred and persecution of Christians, exiled John to the small island of Patmos. It is located southwest of Ephesus, in the Aegean Sea. Even though he was in his late eighties or early nineties, John was forced to work in a marble mine for about a year. Many died from the dangerous, merciless, exhausting slave labor, yet elderly John survived. Spiritually, he did far more than survive. He thrived. John received the Revelation during that time of exile.[1]

The Apostle John was persecuted for his faithfulness to Jesus Christ, but he did not complain about his circumstances (Rev. 1:9 NIV). He had something far better to communicate (verses 10–11). Christ's love for the church is the best model for a Christian marriage."

Revelation

Revelation chapter 1 gives a sneak-peak into the heavenly realm. Jesus Christ is unveiled in His present-day glory. He is no longer a baby in a manger. He is no longer a suffering-servant, hanging on a cross. The description of his clothes, his hair, his eyes, his voice, all vividly declare that he is now the risen, exalted, glorified Lord of the universe (verses 13–18 NIV). As such, however, He is not a distant, detached monarch. Rather, he remains the Lord and master who is with His people. He is among His churches (verses 12, 19–20 NIV).

Revelation 2 and 3 record Jesus Christ's direct communication to his bride, the church. In fact, there were seven of them, all precious to Him. He knew what was happening among His people. He knew the good and the bad. He praised the good and corrected the bad.

Romance

The first church Jesus Christ addressed was the church at Ephesus (Rev. 2:1–7 NIV). The church members were good people. They worked hard and lived right. They believed the right stuff, but they had a problem. Their heads were right, but their hearts were wrong. They had left their first love. As the "Righteous Brothers" used to sing, they had "lost that lovin' feelin'"; it was "gone, gone, gone." And may I remind you, a church without a passionate love for Jesus Christ is in trouble. It may look right, act right, and talk right, but it is an empty shell. So, Jesus Christ Himself dictated a letter to John, and John sent it to the church family in Ephesus.

Geographically, Ephesus was the closest city to the Isle of Patmos. Also, it was John's home church. He had been their pastor. It makes sense that Jesus would write to them first.

First Love

The Christians at Ephesus were previously known for their passionate love for Jesus Christ and for one another.

The Apostle Paul wrote to them in their early days, "For this reason, ever since I heard about your faith in the Lord Jesus and *your love* for all the saints, I have not stopped giving thanks for you, remembering you in my prayers" (Ephesians 1:15–16 NIV). No doubt, John, the Apostle of love, had led them in keeping their love for Jesus vibrant when he was their pastor. They knew intense love. They had lived out love in practical ways. But they left it.

About now you may be thinking, "Forrest, you forgot your subject. You started writing a chapter about romance in our marriages, got distracted, and started writing about a church's love for Jesus." If that is your line of thought, I commend you for being observant. But I assure you, I'm still on course. Do you remember reading Ephesians 5:25–29 NIV?

> *Husbands*, love your *wives*, just as *Christ* loved the *church* and gave himself up for her to make her holy, cleansing her by the washing with water through the word, and to present her to himself as a radiant *church*, without stain or wrinkle or any other blemish, but holy and blameless. In this same way, *husbands* ought to love their *wives* as their own bodies. He who loves his *wife* loves himself. After all, no one ever hated his own body, but he feeds and cares for it, just as *Christ* does the *church*.

The relationship between a husband and wife is an illustration of the relationship between Jesus Christ and His church. So, as we read about how a church can renew a vibrant relationship with Jesus Christ, we will see the way to renew, revive, and revitalize the romance in our marriages.

Maybe you have lost the initial spark that ignited your relationship. Would you say your marriage has severe ignition problems? Consider Jesus' words to the Ephesian believers in Revelation 2:1–5 NIV:

"To the angel of the church in Ephesus write:"

Time out.

The Greek word translated "angel" means "messenger." Here, Jesus is most likely addressing His letter to the pastor ... the God-appointed messenger to the congregation. The pastor, in turn, would deliver the message to the church.

Time in.

"These are the words of him who holds the seven stars in his right hand and walks among the seven golden lampstands:"

Time out again. Let's put on our decoder rings and see if we can figure out what in the world the "seven stars" and "seven golden lampstands" represent. The answer is found in Revelation 1:20 NIV. Jesus tells us exactly what He's talking about.

> "The mystery of the seven stars that you saw in my right hand and of the seven golden lampstands is this: The seven stars are the angels of the seven churches, and the seven lampstands are the seven churches."

Jesus addressed the "stars"—pastors—who will share these letters with their "lampstands"—congregations. Does that mean these Scriptures don't apply to us? Absolutely not. At the end of each of the seven letters to the churches,

Jesus noted the broader audience. He said, "He who has an ear, let him hear what the Spirit says to the churches" (Rev. 2:7a, 11a, 17a, 29; 3:6, 13, 22).

So, if you have an ear, if you are willing to hear and obey; these letters are for you. You see, the seven churches represent the seven kinds of Christians who make up the seven churches. In every church there are some Ephesian Christians who have left their first love, some Smyrna Christians who are faithful in spite of persecution, some Laodicean Christians who are lukewarm in their walk, and right on down the line.

Time in. In chapter 2 verse 2, Jesus begins by giving the believers a compliment:

> [2]"I know your deeds, your hard work and your perseverance. I know that you cannot tolerate wicked men, that you have tested those who claim to be apostles but are not, and have found them false. [3]You have persevered and have endured hardships for my name, and have not grown weary."

Jesus praised them. He was pleased with the church's hard work and faithfulness. But then the hammer fell. His compliment was followed by a correction…

[4]"Yet I hold this against you: You have forsaken your first love. [5]Remember the height from which you have fallen! Repent and do the things you did at first. If you do not repent, I will come to you and remove your lampstand from its place."

At the time John wrote the Revelation, Ephesus had quite a history of Christian activity. It was the mother church to all the Asian churches. Their membership role was a "Who's Who" of New Testament Christianity. Two of their former pastors, Paul and John, wrote no less than eighteen of the twenty-seven books of the New Testament.

- Priscilla and Aquila went to Ephesus with Paul, gave their loyal support, and promoted the Gospel. The church likely began in their house (Acts 18 NIV).

- Apollos, a converted Jew who was mighty in the Scriptures and well known for his eloquent declaration of Jesus Christ, ignited the Ephesian church with his burning zeal. Aquila and Priscilla mentored him at Ephesus.

- Paul preached and ministered to the people of Ephesus for three years, until he was forced to leave the city because of a riot (Acts 19 NIV).

- Upon Paul's departure, young Timothy became the faithful Pastor of the church (1 Timothy 1:3 NIV). Two New Testament books were written to Timothy.

- The Apostle John pastored the church and made it the home base for his evangelistic and teaching tours for several years.

- Mary, the mother of Jesus, who was entrusted to John's care (John 19:26–27 NIV), was also a member of the church in Ephesus.

Wow! What a heritage! But in spite of these high-profile members and achievements, something happened along the way. As impossible as it may seem, this church's love for Jesus Christ waned. They had not *lost* their love; they had *left* it. Jesus had taken second place in their church.

The Ephesian believers' hearts had grown cold. Now, that doesn't mean they didn't love Jesus anymore. They did. But they did not love Him like they used to. The spiritual honeymoon was over.

Maybe you can identify with the Ephesians. Does their church atmosphere remind you of your marriage? It isn't that you don't love your spouse...you've just left your first love¾you don't love him or her as you once did. You have a great history together...but the spark has cooled. You've fallen into a rut. Life together is more routine than romance.

I regularly meet married couples who behave more like roommates than romantics. They share a house, they share a bed, they share a checking account, but they've left their first love. The romance is gone between the bride and the groom.

Jesus has a word of encouragement for the Ephesian church, and for us, if we have ears to hear. Love doesn't have to languish. Love can be revived and renewed. Jesus outlines how to fall in love all over again.

But before we get to the *how* of romance, I need to help you recognize the *what* of romance. It is vital to recognize romance for what it's *not* as well as for what it *is*.

How to Recognize Romance

Three facts will help you recognize romance.

Romance ≠ Sex

First, romance is not the same as sex. You can have a romantic marriage even if one of you is a paraplegic.

Don't equate romance with sex. When you are romantic, you should never have an ulterior motive. Gentlemen, every wife in the world knows the difference between affection, *period*, and affection, *comma*. The affection that satisfies your wife's desire has no strings attached.

Columnist Ann Landers asked her predominantly female readership: "Would you be content to be held close and treated tenderly and forget about 'the act'?" She was swamped with 100,000 replies within four days. The overwhelming response (72%) was, "Yes, I would be content to just snuggle."

A hug is a hug, *period*. It should have no ulterior motives. Husband, when you hug your wife, does she have a reason to be suspicious? Does she wonder, "Is he feeling frisky, or did he just buy a new boat?"

The husband who seldom touches his wife—except as an entree to lovemaking—needs to understand something. He is depriving his wife of the knowledge that she is loved and appreciated, *period*. Gentlemen, believe it or not, that knowledge is as important to her as sex is to you. If you haven't learned this principle, you are on the fast track to resentment and miscommunication. Equating romance and sex tends to turn romance into bartering.

Are you beginning to recognize romance? Romance is not the same as sex.

Romance: Creative ≠ Compulsory

Second, creative romance is not the same as compulsory romance.

Compulsory Romance

Compulsory romance occurs on those occasions when you must be romantic… *or else.* For example, a card and a nice gift are compulsory to celebrate her birthday. She may tell you, "Ah honey, don't get me anything this year." But she doesn't mean it.

He may tell you not to bother getting him a gift for Christmas… but just do it one year. He'll never forgive you. It's compulsory.

When anniversary time comes around, you'd better be prepared to do something romantic. And when Valentine's Day arrives, you'd better have more than a salad shooter, a dust-buster, a weed whacker, a deluxe iron, or five gallons of drywall compound to give. Romance on Valentine's Day is compulsory.

Men can bellyache about compulsory romance. But it's never going to change.

I'm your friend, let me break the bad news to you: *You don't get any points for buying roses or jewelry or cards or candy for compulsory occasions.* I know, it isn't fair. It isn't right. But it is the truth¾so get over it.

If you fail to present the appropriate gift on a compulsory day, it will cost you. A man once said, "A sure fire way to remember your wife's birthday is… just forget it once."

Creative Romance

But not all the news is negative. It is possible to transform compulsory romance into creative romance. What turns the compulsory romance days into romantic events? Little surprises.

Exercise a little creativity. On Valentines Day, don't send roses ... everybody does that. Besides, roses are expensive in February. Instead, buy her tulips ... and attach a note: "I've got two-lips waiting for you!"

One year I lined our driveway with signs that proclaimed, "I love Dawn Pollock."

Hire a chef. Have him or her cook a romantic dinner in your home. I did that once.

You are creative in every other area of your life. Why not apply it to your marriage? Be creative.

We have noted two things that romance "is not." Romance "is not" the same as sex. Creative romance "is not" the same as compulsory romance. Now, notice what "is" romantic. It is important to understand that ...

Spouse Defines Romance

Third, your spouse defines what *is* romantic. If you give her flowers, and she hates flowers, it ain't romantic. If you've spent all day cooking a gourmet meal, and he'd rather call Domino's for a pizza ... guess what? It isn't romantic. If you've spent a fortune on an outfit for her, and she says it isn't her style, you have no right to be resentful.

One writer tells the story of Bob and Betty. In their early years together, Bob and Betty stumbled onto a practice that revolutionized their marriage. They asked each other, "What says, 'I love you' *to you?*"

Betty had long assumed that, more than anything else, Bob wanted the house immaculately clean when he arrived home from work. Every afternoon, as his arrival time approached, she rushed through the house like a whirlwind, cleaning everything in sight.

Betty always greeted Bob at the door. She then followed him into the house waiting for his praise. Since she had made the extra effort to have a clean house, just like he wanted, she thought the least he could do was notice and appreciate her work. But the praise never came. Understandably, seeds of resentment took root, grew, and bloomed in Betty's heart. Bob obviously suffered from an acute case of insensitivity. He was a demanding ingrate.

One day she'd had enough. With fire in her eyes, she confronted Bob. As they talked, Betty discovered that Bob really didn't care if the house was clean when he got home. He just wanted to know what was for dinner! The meal didn't have to be ready; they could be ordering pizza for all he cared. A clean house did not say, "I love you" to Bob. He wanted a happy wife with dinner plans.

Betty and Bob's assumptions robbed both of them. Her frantic house cleaning kept her from dinner plans and preparations. His expectation of dinner plans and preparation distracted him from praising her immaculate care for their home. They were in a vicious cycle. Neither was satisfied because both made false assumptions.

Is it possible that some of your frustrations with your spouse are being watered and fertilized by false assumptions? Let your spouse tell you what is romantic. He or she knows, and you can reap the rewards.

1. Romance "is not" the same as sex.

2. Creative romance "is not" the same as compulsory romance.

3. Your spouse defines what "is" romantic.

The Ephesian Church had neglected some things in their relationship with Jesus Christ that caused them to forsake their first love. Likewise, husbands and wives neglect some things that ruin romance.

How to Ruin Romance

Romance isn't ruined overnight. Just as the Ephesians didn't ruin their relationship with Christ overnight; walls are built, brick by brick, over time. Bad experiences accumulate through the years. The bricks in a relationship barrier are held together with the mortar of indifference.

Jesus warned the Ephesians that they had forsaken their first love. The same can happen in a marriage.

At least three things can ruin romance. See if you recognize any or all of these in your relationship.

Neglect

First, neglect ruins romance. I'm reminded of the old joke about the fellow who didn't kiss his wife for eighteen years, but shot the first man who did. You can't neglect your spouse indefinitely without both husband and wife paying a price.

A survey in 2007 revealed that 65 percent of the respondents spent more time at home with their computer than with their spouse.[2] It is now possible to have more communication with someone in Outer Mongolia than with a spouse in the next room.

Are you familiar with "entropy"? The *American Heritage Dictionary* offers multiple shades of meaning. In thermodynamics it refers to the amount of energy within a closed system that is unavailable to do work. Another meaning is a measure of the loss of information in a transmitted message. Has neglect caused you and your spouse to suffer from communication entropy? Do you regularly complete a conversation with your spouse and then wonder if she told you something important? Entropy also refers to the inevitable and steady deterioration of a system or society.

All of the definitions of entropy refer to unavailable or lost energy and information. As a result, anything affected by entropy tends to weaken, deteriorate, and run down. Entropy is the assumed, inevitable result of neglect.

Beware of the phenomenon of "Relationship Entropy"—the tendency of relationships to become more diluted if not cared-for and nurtured; lovers who were once close, tend to drift apart if both partners do not work at the relationship on a consistent basis. Neglect leads to taking each other for granted.

According to Revelation 2:3 NIV, the Ephesian church had endured hardships. Maybe they were persecuted for their faith. Maybe they had struggled to survive. But whatever the cause … they had neglected their first love. Neglect ruins romance.

Financial Pressure and Stress

Second, financial pressure and stress can ruin romance. Experienced divorce lawyers were asked to list the most common cause for divorce that they observed in their practices. Their top five list was:

#5 Infidelity,
#4 A dramatic change in priorities,
#3 A lack of commitment to the marriage,
#2 Financial problems, and …
#1 Poor communication.[3]

Recently, a survey in Los Angeles County sought both the happiest and the unhappiest families in the county. An interesting discovery was made. The unfortunate family who received "the unhappy family award" had an annual income of over $500,000. They lived in a fabulous house, but were overwhelmed with financial pressures. The only discernable feelings between the husband and wife were bitterness and cynicism. Their children were steadily progressing from bad to worse. Confusion and bickering dominated the atmosphere of this affluent home. The survey concluded, "This is the most unhappy home we could find."

In contrast, the happiest home was discovered in a mobile home park. The husband was crippled; the wife was arthritic. They had a teenage daughter, but they had no financial problems. Frugal management of meager finances allowed the family to live comfortably on his part-time night watchman's income. The home was filled with laughter and joy and fun and humor; the atmosphere overflowed with love.

Financial pressures often ruin romance. But notice, the amount of financial stress is not determined by the level of one's income. Financial stress is determined by the management of one's financial outgo.

Unresolved Anger and Hurt

Third, unresolved anger and hurt can ruin romance. Conflict is impossible to avoid, but it is not impossible to resolve. If you deal with conflict in the right way, tensions are calmed. If you deal with conflict in the wrong way, tension builds in the home until you progress through four stages of hurt. Each stage can lead to greater alienation between a husband and wife.

Four Stages of Heart Hurt

The Wounded Heart

We all know something about this stage. Our mates have wounded us, and we've wounded them. Sometimes it happens intentionally, sometimes unintentionally. If we're sensitive at all, we pick up our mate's signals and know when he or she feels wounded. We know when something's wrong, when things have gotten out of balance. No married person can honestly say, "I've never known anything about the wounded heart."

Ignore the wounded heart long enough and it turns into something else.

The Cold Heart

During the second stage, a husband might recognize his wife's wounded heart and begin to talk to her, but without trying to resolve the conflict. Communication takes place, but it lacks any power to resolve the dispute. The couple may act indifferent toward each other. He's Mr. Cool; she's Mrs. Unflustered. "The conflict doesn't bother me!" As they avoid the issue and any meaningful contact with each other, the cold heart sets in.

The Hard Heart

The third stage reflects serious trouble. In the hard-hearted stage, you grieve the Holy Spirit. You do what God said not to do. "And do not grieve the Holy Spirit of God, with whom you were sealed for the day of redemption" (Ephesians 4:30 NIV). As a result, you have trouble praying. That's why the apostle Peter urged, "Husbands, in the same way be considerate as you live with your wives, and treat them with respect as the weaker partner and as heirs with you of the gracious gift of life, so that nothing will hinder your prayers" (1 Peter 3:7 NIV). When you're not in a right relationship with your mate, heaven seems blocked and God seems far away. At the hard-heart stage, you're metallic and tough. As you go through the motions, you begin to wonder if your marriage will last. All kinds of conflict may break loose, but you're so hard and cold and businesslike you really don't care.

And that leads to the fourth, and fatal, stage.

The Apathetic Heart

The opposite of love is not hate. The opposite of love is apathy; it's indifference, an "I don't care" attitude.

Through the years I've counseled many couples. Unfortunately, it is not uncommon for a man to bitterly declare his hatred for his wife. His wife usually has equal venom. They tell me what they can't stand, and what they justly despised about their spouse.

When a pastoral counseling session starts down the "I despise…" and "I can't stand it when…" road, I am encouraged. I know what to do. I listen awhile. I let him talk out his anger. Sometimes it's more spewed out than talked out. I let the hurting husband say enough to be ready to listen. Then, I look him in the eyes as if I'm looking into his heart (because I am), and I say, "You *really* love her, don't you!" Almost without fail the husband looks astonished and asks, "How could you tell?" Easy. The anger has revealed his heart. There's hope for such a man or woman. He or she still cares enough to be emotionally involved and to want their relationship to be better.

But there is little hope for the couple who is apathetic and indifferent. He doesn't care—neither does she. They no longer have an emotional investment in the relationship. Love is gone and the marriage is withered, if not dead.

How tragic! And it's even more tragic when the marriage plummeted to the fourth stage over trivial conflicts that simply spiraled out of proportion.

So, now that we know how to recognize romance and ruin romance … let's think about …

How to Reignite Romance

Once love dies, can it be resurrected? Can love be reborn? You bet.

Jesus warned the church at Ephesus, "You have forsaken your first love" (Rev. 2:4 NIV). Apparently it had happened without their realizing it. So, Jesus gave them a four-step process for re-igniting the relationship they once enjoyed with Him.

"First love" is genuine "romantic love." The Church at Ephesus had left their romantic love for the Lord. What was true of the Church at Ephesus is true of many marriages. The romance is gone.

Notice four principles for rekindling the romance in your relationship.

Step 1: Realize

Realize there is a problem. Like the Ephesian church, some couples don't even realize they have a problem. More often, however, only one of the spouses will be clueless. If you want to know whether or not you have forsaken your first love, ask your spouse. He or she knows.

I meet couples who confess that they simply co-exist. They live together out of habit, convenience, and economic necessity. They have become comfortable roommates. She lives her life and he lives his. But there's no real relationship. The romance, the chemistry, is missing.

Sometimes it takes thirty years for a relationship to fall into such a rut. Sometimes it happens in three.

I once spoke with a man who had been married for three years. He said that he and his wife had not been intimate, even one time, since their honeymoon night. They were roommates. They loved one another, but the passion was gone.

Other men are oblivious to the absence of romance in their marriages. I know such a man; I'll call him Bill. He went on a week long deer hunting trip. When Bill returned home, his wife, his kids, all of their furniture, and all of the money in his bank account were gone.

Bill was shocked. He hadn't noticed a problem. Over the preceding seventeen years, incrementally and almost imperceptibly, the two had drifted apart. They didn't continue their courtship after marriage; they didn't go on dates anymore; they never got away for a romantic weekend, just the two of them. Instead, they had fallen into a rut, which is really a grave with both ends knocked out. Their marriage died, but he didn't notice.

If many men and women gave the same attention to their careers that they give to their marriages, they would be unemployed, unemployable, bankrupt, and homeless. How about you?

Jesus said, ⁴"Yet I hold this against you: You have forsaken your first love."The Ephesian believers didn't know they had a problem either. These words must have been like cold water in their faces. They were busy doing things for God. They were worshipping. They were singing hymns. They were serving. They were going through the motions, and yet, the passion was gone.

For many, re-igniting your romantic relationship will require a realization that something is wrong in the first place.

You say, "Well, how can I find out if my marriage is healthy or not?" Again, ASK.

A good friend of mine does a courageous thing each year. He sits down with his wife and asks her nine questions. As he does, he offers no arguments, corrections, or excuses. He merely listens and takes notes.

Nine Courageous Questions

1. What can I do to make you feel more loved?

2. What can I do to give you confidence I respect you and the desires of your heart?

3. What can I do to help you feel more secure?

> 4. What can I do to prove I have heard and understand your heart?
>
> 5. What can I do to give you greater confidence in our future together?
>
> 6. Is there an attribute of mine that I can improve?
>
> 7. Is there an attribute of yours that I can help you improve?
>
> 8. What can I do to demonstrate my desire to be more like Christ?
>
> 9. What mutual goal would you like us to have?

Step 2: Remember

Remember how it used to be. To rekindle the relationship, Jesus told the Ephesians to... ⁵"Remember the height from which you have fallen!"

The Ephesians had once been passionately in love with Jesus Christ. They had fallen head over heels for Him. They had forsaken all the false gods of the Greek world for the one true and living God. Those first years had been thrilling. But the thrill was gone and the boring routine had set in.

Jesus said, "Remember how you used to be..."

Do you remember when you were first married? You would sit for hours and just talk. Meals at restaurants were not consumed in silence. You looked at one another instead of scanning the crowd and the horizon. Sir, do you remember when you just listened to her? You didn't try to problem-solve; you didn't try to give advice; you didn't agree or disagree. You just listened. And by listening, you validated her.

Often, when men think women are looking for answers, they're simply looking for *compassion and understanding*.

Do you remember when you first got married? Your bedchamber was a place of romance. It was your own personal, private, romantic hide-away. But today...it looks like an all-purpose room. On one side of the room, the TV blares with *American Idol*. On the other side of the room, your exercise equipment gathers dust, except for the places were it is used as a clothes horse.

Get rid of that TV! Take the exercise bike to the garage. You won't miss it. Dim the lights. Put some flowers on the nightstand. Remember how you used to behave toward one another when you first married.

And do you remember when you were dating? You would volunteer to do things with each other that you wouldn't do with anyone else if they paid you. And you did them cheerfully, just so you could be together. Why not try some of those things again?

Husbands:
- Maybe you could go dress shopping with her.
- Maybe you could attend the ballet with her.

Wives:
- Maybe you could do some gardening with him.
- Maybe you could watch some sports with him.

Don't force him to choose between you and his golf, football, basketball, cars, or fishing! As they say, "If you can't beat 'em, join 'em!" Read a book about his favorite sport-hobby-pastime so you can join in, or at least understand what's going on.

Doing things together is more important than what you do. Don't position yourself against his or her passions.

Remember how you used to behave before you got married? Realize, remember, and...

Step 3: Repent

Jesus summed it up nicely. He said, "Repent..." Repentance is a change of mind (you think a new way), a change of heart (you have new desires), that leads to a change of actions (you put those new thoughts and desires into action).

Do something different. Change your habits. Climb out of the rut. Embrace a new passion for your husband or wife. Which brings us to...

Step 4: Return

Jesus said, "Repent and do the things you did at first."

Is that an appropriate exhortation for you? Do you need the reminder to do things you did at the first... such as act like a gentleman?

Gentlemen, there is a small fringe of feminist extremists who wouldn't want you to open a door for them if the building was on fire. But you're not married to one of them. Your wife loves a real gentleman. So repent and revive chivalry.

- Open her car door. Don't just open the door when your car is new. Open it every time. Treat your wife like the relationship is new.

- Hold the chair for her at dinner.

- Help her as she puts on her coat.

Your wife will warm up to you romantically and otherwise when she sees a revival of manners.

And all the women said, "Amen."

But ladies, you don't get off the hook. Some of you need to repent and return. Start gussying yourself up like you used to. Remember when he was coming to pick you up for a date" and you spent two hours doing your hair, your nails, and picking out just the right outfit. You sprayed on the perfume. When he stood on the porch with that silly grin and bouquet of roses, he said, "Hey honey love, you look fine," because you did.

If your husband comes home every day to find you looking like a bale of hay shot out of a cannon, your bathrobe singed in the middle, cream and goo smeared all over your face, and scrap-iron in your hair, he'll watch TV until his eyes glaze over. At least, he will if he is half-way smart.

And all the men said, "Amen."

Jesus, the creator of the universe, said, "Get back to the basics. I know you've been distracted. I know you've been discouraged. I know you've been disheartened. But start showing your love like you used to."

The sad truth is, there is *The Romantic Law of Inverse Proportions*. It states, "The more you need romance in your life, the less likely you are to have it; and, the less you need it, the more likely you are to have it." But if you'll take action, beginning today, you can re-ignite romance in your home.

The little things you do will signal your desire to return to the way things used to be. Little gifts, and the creativity you show in getting them, will communicate volumes.

A wife knew her husband loved Beethoven. She purchased CDs of all nine symphonies, along with nine red roses, nine balloons, and wrote nine little love notes. That's not expensive … but it is creative. It showed her husband something new was afoot.

If your spouse likes Mozart, you'll have to buy forty-two symphonies. And if it's Haydn he loves, you're *really* in trouble. Papa Haydn composed an incredible 108 symphonies! But the point is, be creative.

When traveling, give her a rose for each day you'll be away.

Maybe you could renew your wedding vows.

In 2000, Dawn and I celebrated our 10th wedding anniversary. It just so happened that we were in Oklahoma City that year for Thanksgiving, which coincidentally fell right on our anniversary. Weeks in advance, I contacted Dawn's mother. We conspired to recreate our wedding day. We reserved the same sanctuary we had used ten years before. I twisted the arm of our former pastor to come perform the wedding ceremony on Thanksgiving Day. We rented little tuxedos for our three boys and little bridesmaids' dresses for our three girls. My mother-in-law got a wedding dress for Dawn.

That evening her mother made up a story about needing to drop by the church to pick up something. When they arrived in the sanctuary, there we stood waiting. The party was small—the preacher and the eight of us in a room that would seat 5500.

The music started playing while Dawn changed clothes. Soon she retraced her steps down the aisle, and we renewed our vows.

That evening, we stayed in the same hotel where we had spent our honeymoon night. And, no, we didn't take the children.

As a Visa commercial would sum it up...

- Formal clothes for the kids, $300

- Cake at the reception, $55

- Room at the hotel where we had our honeymoon, $150

- Telling your bride you'd marry her all over again ... Priceless.

A Romantic Conclusion

The nearest thing to heaven on earth is a marriage where a husband and wife live in love and peace together for the Lord and each other. The nearest thing to hell on earth is a marriage where two people bicker and quarrel, or worse yet ... ignore one another like ships passing in the night.

Jesus wants you to experience love like it was intended to be. He is the greatest lover of all time. The Bible says, "God is love" (1 John 4:16 NIV). But God's love is more than mere talk. "God demonstrates his own love for us in this: while we were still sinners, Christ died for us" (Romans 5:8 NIV).

Jesus not only felt love for us; he showed love to us. He put his love into action.

Dear friend, perhaps you were saved a long time ago … you came into a relationship with Christ. It's real. It's genuine. But you've forsaken your first love. Right now, you could give your heart back to him. Realize there is a problem. Remember how it used to be. Repent. Return. he will welcome you.

If, on the other hand, you have never begun a personal relationship with Jesus Christ, he is proposing a relationship with you right now. All you have to do is go to Jesus Christ by faith. He loves you. He endured the punishment for all of your sins when he suffered and died on the cross. He was buried and rose from the dead on the third day. His resurrection proves God is completely satisfied with his sacrifice. There is nothing else for you to do, but accept him by faith.

Are you now willing to accept Jesus Christ as your Lord and Savior? Then tell him that you accept His proposal. Express your faith by a simple prayer like this: "Lord Jesus, I am a sinner. I cannot save myself, but I trust you to save me. Come into my heart. Be my savior and Lord. I believe you died for me. I believe you were buried and rose from the dead, and I believe you are alive today. I trust you. I receive you into my life. Give me the power to live for you. In Jesus' name, amen."

The Lying King
Hebrews 13:4

What can you do if trust has been broken between you and your spouse? If you discover you are married to *the lying king*... or *queen*, what can you do? Is there any hope for your marriage if your spouse has had an affair?

Surely no groom marries, intending to break his vows. Surely no bride in her demure veil and elegant wedding dress is making plans to destroy her life as she walks to the marriage altar on her father's arm. Couples marry with the best intentions. Yet, adultery is rampant. Obviously something happens along the way to sabotage good intentions.

The first time I came face to face with the devastation of adultery is engraved into my memory. I was a young kid working at a television station in Oklahoma City. We were in the middle of a live broadcast of the ten o'clock nightly news. The news anchor looked into the camera and teased the next segment, "Stay right there. Sports is up next with our own...," and he named the sports anchor. We went into a commercial.

I was in the control booth looking at the preview monitor... and to my horror, the sports anchor's chair was empty. The producer went into virtual seizures, yelling frantically, "Where is he?! Where is he?!"

He turned to me and said, "Forrest, you're on! Do the Sports. Save our broadcast! We're counting on you."

Just kidding. This wasn't a movie; it was reality.

The producer turned to me and yelled, "Forrest, go find him! Quick! We're on a two minute break!"

I bolted out of the control booth and ran furiously all over the station... the newsroom, the coffee shop, the offices. Finally, with just seconds remaining, I ran to the receptionist desk. And there he was... in the arms of the young receptionist. He had been there all the time and had missed his cue.

That night, when the newscast was over, I saw that same sports anchor put on his overcoat to go out into the rain. His wife was waiting outside in their station wagon. His two school-age boys were in the back seat.

I stood there in disbelief... and wanted to vomit.

Believe it or not, the sacred intimacy of your marriage matters to God. The Creator of marriage (Genesis 2) declared, "Marriage should be honored by *all*, and the marriage bed kept pure, for God will judge the adulterer and all the sexually immoral" (Hebrews 13:4 NIV).

God is not prudish; he is protective. "The marriage bed" is a metaphor for the sex act between a husband and a wife. The Greek word translated "pure," means *unstained by sin.*

Sexual relations between a husband and wife are honorable and holy. Husbands and wives can celebrate the first half of the verse, "Marriage should be honored by all, and the marriage bed kept pure." But don't overlook the second half, "God will judge the adulterer and all the sexually immoral." Anyone who desecrates God's precious and pure gift will answer to him.

The Bible's warning against adultery is vivid and urgent. It compares adultery to a trap.[1] One who is seduced into adultery is like an ox entering a slaughter house. An adulterer is like a deer caught in a trap, soon to be shot through the liver with an arrow. He or she is like a bird darting into a snare (Proverbs 7:21–23 NIV). Unfortunately, many husbands and wives unwittingly rush into the trap. They seem oblivious to the destruction awaiting them. And the collateral damage is equally devastating. The landscape is littered with broken homes, abandoned husbands, and single moms. Worst of all, adultery has produced a generation of emotionally scared, latchkey kids; and most of them are living in poverty.

So let's first consider...

The Problem of Adultery

The word "adultery" means an illicit sexual relationship between a married person and one to whom he or she is not married.[2] It is the root word of "adulterate," which means *to contaminate*, and that identifies the problem. Marriage is pure. Adultery contaminates marriage.

When something is adulterated, an impure and inferior substance is mixed with a pure and superior substance.[3]

That's exactly what adultery is and does: the impurity of sexual immorality is mixed with the purity of the marriage bed (Heb. 13:4 NIV). The adulterated result is not only diluted and inferior...it is deadly and deserves God's judgment.

The devil has conducted a remarkably effective campaign to introduce adultery into homes all over America. Because of the devastating results, allow me to unveil the seven primary tools he uses to adulterate erstwhile happy marriages.[4] Observe and be warned.

The first destructive tool is...

Unsatisfied Needs

A man and woman meet, fall in love, and marry. Both begin marriage with the hope and expectation that their needs will be met.

Perhaps you feel all of your needs are being met by your marital relationship. Wonderful. But the more important question is...are the needs of your spouse being met? Are you meeting your spouse's needs for acceptance, attention, and affection?

When needs go unmet in marriage, people naturally seek to satisfy their needs elsewhere. Beware. If either partner's emotional, physical or sexual needs are not being met in your marriage, you are prime targets for adultery.

Unmet Expectations

Harlequin and Hollywood have bequeathed to us larger-than-life expectations for weddings and marriage. It's all supposed to be a fairytale:

- Boy meets girl—it's love at first sight.

- He's as handsome as George Clooney.

- She's a perpetual size four and could have been a fashion model.

- A steamy courtship culminates in a fairytale wedding.

- And they live happily ever after, waltzing in the ballroom of their castle.

That's the fantasy, and people are willing to pay a lot for a fantasy. The average cost for a wedding nowadays is $16,485. Castles are considerably more.

If a couple assumes marriage will be a perpetual *Harlequin Romance*, each day attended by roses, valentines, and bubble baths, they will have unmet expectations. Guaranteed.

Unmet expectations can transform a husband or wife into a prime candidate for adultery. Why? Into the gap between expectations and reality, a special someone inevitably appears. She may arrive at the office. He may stroll casually into the Country Club. You may meet him or her at church or the PTF. The place is not important; it is the unmet expectations that make you vulnerable.

Third, adultery starts because of…

Underdeveloped Self-Esteem

In a pre-marital counseling session I ask young couples, "Why are you getting married?" Some respond, "Because he makes me happy," or, "Because I feel good about myself when we're together." You may think that sounds sweet. Years of pastoral counseling make me think, "Uh-oh!"

I see a giant red flag waving when someone claims he or she is getting married because of what the other person provides. Allow me to interpret. They're saying, "I have a perpetual itch, and I expect this person to scratch it for the rest of my life." The unspoken agreement is that as long as my needs are satisfied, as long as my spouse holds up his or her end of the bargain, I'll stick around. But the moment the relationship no longer benefits me, *"Hasta la vista, baby."*

If you believe getting married will be self-actualizing or will make you feel more secure, happy, or at peace with yourself, you are in for a big shock. Sooner or later someone who seems better equipped to service your self-esteem will come along. You will then be a prime target for adultery.

A fourth reason for adultery is...

Unresolved Conflict

Conflict is not bad, necessarily. In fact, some conflict may be healthy. As I previously noted, if two people agree on everything, one of them isn't necessary. The right kind of conflict can clarify your thinking and help you make course corrections. A proper response to conflict can strengthen your marriage.

Unresolved conflict is different. Unresolved conflict inflicts wounds that fester rather than heal.

For a variety of reasons, both biological and cultural, men have a harder time handling conflict. Women have a harder time tolerating emotional distance. Thus, men often *withdraw* from conflict while women *confront* conflict. Men think, if we can avoid talking about it, it'll be okay. In contrast, women think if we can discuss it openly, thoroughly, and repeatedly, we can resolve it. The more she tries to confront, the more he tries to withdraw. The more he tries to withdraw, the more she tries to confront. And the vicious cycle ignites anger.

Anger harbored day-to-day and week-to-week grows into a mountain of unresolved conflict, and the mountain will not be removed easily. Eventually someone will appear to listen and share your anger. Before you realize it, the new friend's understanding and compassion will escalate your anger toward your spouse ("Why can't my husband listen like he does?"), and deepen your infatuation with your new friend ("Why can't my wife be more like her? She's the kind of woman I really need."). Too often, such a friend becomes a lover.

A fifth destructive tool the enemy uses to adulterate marriage is ...

Unexpected Mortality

Psychologists call this the "midlife crisis." Its symptoms are deeply felt but often unrecognized. One "expert" stated:

If you are going through midlife crisis, you might experience a wide range of feelings, such as:

- Discontent with life and/or the lifestyle that may have provided happiness for many years
- Boredom with things/people that have hitherto held great interest and dominated your life

- Feeling adventurous and wanting to do something completely different
- Questioning the meaning of life, and the validity of decisions clearly and easily made years before
- Confusion about who you are, or where your life is going.[5]

One day the fellow who has always prided himself on his athletic build looks in a full-length mirror and sees balding and bulging. At least he can see them when he wears his bifocals.

A woman looks in the mirror and her mother looks back. Lines and wrinkles seem to have appeared overnight. She tries to cover them with cosmetics. (By the way, did you know that our English word "cosmetics" comes from the Greek word "cosmos," which means to bring order to chaos?) The mirror tells her that gravity is taking over. She may have a face-lift or chin-lift or an eye-lift. Pretty soon, she's had so many plastic surgeries, when she sits down, her mouth snaps open!

In the midst of this midlife crisis, a charming, attractive, appealing guy at the office comments on her youthfulness and attractiveness. Some sweet hard-body at the gym comments on how handsome he is … and the flames of passion are ignited.

Unexpected mortality gives you a choice. Will you make a desperate attempt to recapture your youth? Or, will you allow your realization of mortality to draw you closer to God? Will you succumb to the panic of your midlife crisis? Or, will you realize, "The length of our days is seventy years—or eighty, if we have the strength;...for they quickly pass, and we fly away....Teach us to number our days aright, that we may gain a heart of wisdom" (Psalm 90:10, 12 NIV). "A short life should be wisely spent."[6] Such wisdom will insulate you against adultery.

Another all too common cause of adultery is the failure to exercise common sense around the opposite sex. I'll call this...

Unguarded Encounters

Adultery can occur simply because you do not exercise caution. Don't misunderstand. It isn't that you are irresistible. The devil just happens to hate Jesus, the family, and you that much. He wants to dishonor Jesus, destroy your family, and silence your witness for Jesus Christ. Remember, adultery is a trap. If you aren't alert, you will be caught in the trap before you realize it.

Ministers especially must beware of unguarded encounters. Years ago I read something called "The Ten Commandments for Maintaining Moral Integrity." I've tried to live by these.

Ten Commandments for Maintaining Ministerial Moral Integrity

1. Thou shalt not visit the opposite sex alone at their home.

2. Thou shalt not counsel the opposite sex alone at the office.

---

3. Thou shalt not counsel the opposite sex more than once without that person's mate. Refer them.

4. Thou shalt not go to lunch alone with the opposite sex.

5. Thou shalt not kiss any attender of the opposite sex or show affection that could be questioned.

6. Thou shalt not discuss detailed sexual problems with the opposite sex in counseling. Refer them.

7. Thou shalt not discuss your marriage problems with an attender of the opposite sex.

8. Thou shalt be careful in answering cards and letters from the opposite sex.

9. Thou shalt make your secretary your protective ally.

10. Thou shalt pray for the integrity of other staff members.

You may think, "Forrest, you're overreacting." No, dear friend... the Bible says, "... among you there must not be even a hint of sexual immorality" (Ephesians 5:3 NIV). For my Lord, my wife, my children, my church, and my eternal accountability for my ministry, I plan to keep it that way.

The seventh destructive tool is...

Unreliable Commitment

Some people enter marriage in a light-hearted, swept-off-their-feet frenzy. They don't think of marriage as a holy relationship that is *for life*. They think of it as more of a serviceable and disposable convenience.

Our Lord Jesus said, "No one who puts his hand to the plow and looks back is fit for service in the kingdom of God" (Luke 9:62 NIV). Jesus spoke of the total commitment that is necessary for Christian service. The same kind of commitment is required for Christian marriage. No "escape clause" is included in God's marriage contract. The world, the flesh, and the devil regularly apply the destructive tool of unreliable commitment to modern marriages.

The enemy of our souls uses seven tools to adulterate previously happy marriages. Be honest with yourself and with God. Do you see any of these tools being used to disassemble and demolish your marriage? If so, you are vulnerable. The problem of adultery may be working its way into your marriage.

Now let's assume for the moment that the worst has happened. You've caught your spouse ... or your spouse has caught you. Guilt is unquestionable. Your marriage is infected with the terminal disease of adultery. Is there any hope? Is there a prescription that might bring healing?

Yes, I'm happy to say there is hope. Honesty, however, compels me to warn that there are no guarantees. With that qualified hope, consider ...

The Prescription for Healing Adultery

If you are involved in adultery now, or have been in the past, there is a pathway to purity. But you must be willing to take the prescription "as directed." And you must take the full dosage. Don't stop taking the antidote when you start feeling better about yourself.

The process of restoration begins with the bitter pill of repentance. In Psalm 51 David repented of his adultery with Bathsheba. He pleaded:

> [1]Have mercy on me, O God, according to your unfailing love; according to your great compassion blot out my transgressions. [2]Wash away all my iniquity and cleanse me from my sin. [3]For I know my transgressions, and my sin is always before me. [4]Against you, you only, have I sinned and done what is evil in your sight, so that you are proved right when you speak and justified when you judge.

David is revered as the greatest of Israel's kings. God called him a man after His own heart (1 Samuel 13:14; Acts 13:22 NIV). This was true, not because he sinned, but in spite of his sin. His adultery was forgiven; it was healed, because he was willing to ...

Repent and Confess the Sin

To whom should you confess your sin? I counsel people to follow a general rule: public sins should be confessed *publicly*. Private sins should be confessed *privately*. The number of people who know about your adultery determines how public your confession must be.

You say, well…why can't we just go on as if it never happened? Because Proverbs 28:13 says, "He who conceals his sins does not prosper, but whoever confesses and renounces them finds mercy."

You need to face up to your sin. You need to own it.

David was restored when he repented and confessed his sin to God. You will be too. As the leader of the nation, David's sin became internationally known. So, he went public with his confession by writing and publishing Psalm 51. The circle of knowledge will determine the extent of your confession. But you cannot avoid the bitter pill of repentance and confession.

Second, genuine repentance requires action. You must…

Run from the Illicit Relationship

The Bible says, "Flee the evil desires of youth" (2 Timothy 2:22 NIV). If you are older, flee those desires, too.

End the illicit relationship. *End it now!* Do not see the partner in sin one last time. Do not make a phone call. Don't meet for lunch. Don't meet in your rendezvous hideaway for "old time's sake." Make it clear by your actions and attitude that the relationship is over. Period.

Joseph is the classic example of fleeing the evil desires of youth (Genesis 39). Joseph was a slave in Egypt. He was smart, well-built and handsome. Potiphar, one of Pharaoh's officials, was his master. Potiphar learned to trust Joseph to run all of his personal business affairs. His business prospered because God's supernatural favor was on Joseph.

Potiphar's wife soon noticed the handsome young slave who efficiently ran things in their mansion. She was accustomed to having anything and everything she wanted, and she added Joseph to her wish list. She lusted for Joseph and propositioned him repeatedly. He respectfully refused and avoided being alone with her. In fact, he worked at staying away from her. Yet, she sought him out and continued to beg him to go to bed with her. She repeatedly made the offer.

Mrs. Potiphar grew tired of a slave treating her like a beggar. On day she took matters into her own hands. She became aggressive. "She caught him by his cloak and said, 'Come to bed with me!'" (Genesis 39:12a NIV).

What did Joseph do? Joseph didn't try to reason or negotiate. He didn't kneel by her bed and say, "Mrs. Potiphar, let's talk about this..." or "Mrs. Potiphar, why don't we meet over supper to work this out." No, the Bible says Joseph evacuated the premises. "He left his cloak in her hand and ran out of the house" (verse 12b). He got out of there faster than a pig at a *Bar Mitzvah*. And you can, too.

If you are in an illicit relationship, repent and *run*. If you are tempted to be in one, *run*. Third ...

Resolve to Avoid Future Contact

In a lengthy passage on adultery the writer of Proverbs emphatically commands, "Keep to a path far from her, do not go near the door of her house," (Proverbs 5:8 NIV). Friend, ending a relationship requires drastic action. That's why you must stop seeing the other person cold-turkey. Cut off contact. Never see the partner in sin again.

Yes, I hear your objections. "But we work in the same place. We have to see one another." All right, get transferred. If necessary, quit your job. If you own the company, call in a favor and have a friend hire her. Whatever it takes, get away; avoid future contact.

"But the other person lives in our neighborhood." Then sell your house! Which is more important, your house … or your home?

"But the other person attends our church." Then for your sake, the sake of your marriage, and the sake of your church, move your membership!

You must flee fornication. Put lots of pavement between you and your accomplice. "Flee the evil desires of youth, and pursue righteousness, faith, love and peace" (2 Timothy 2:22 NIV).

Fourth, you must …

Request Forgiveness

Don't expect or demand your spouse to forgive you overnight, however. Your actions put you into the situation. Don't imagine you can simply talk your way out. God forgives instantly. When you confess (1 John 1:9 NIV), the blood of Jesus Christ cleanses completely (1 John 1:7 NIV). But your spouse is not God. Unquestionable evidence of your repentance must be shown over time.

On the other hand, if you are the victimized party, please do everything within your power to forgive your spouse. If he or she is repentant, has forsaken the adulterous relationship, and requests forgiveness, ask God for the grace to forgive. Be open to the possibility that God can restore your relationship.

Do you stay married? Maybe. Maybe not. I hope you will. The Bible certainly encourages you to stay together; but it does give you the liberty to divorce (Matthew 5:32 NIV). However, for the sake of your mental well-being; forgive. For the sake of your children; forgive.

Nothing good comes from nursing a grudge. In fact, the opposite is true. The Bible says, "See to it that no one misses the grace of God and that no bitter root grows up to cause trouble and defile many" (Hebrews 12:15 NIV). If you do not respond with grace, bitterness will take root in your life. The root will grow and bear fruit, and the fruit will trouble and corrupt the people around you. Think of the bitter people you know. Do you want to be like them? Do you want your children to feel that way about you? Forgiveness is more than a pious suggestion.

Before writing this chapter, I re-read the Bible passages recording Peter's betrayal of Jesus. In Matthew 26 NIV, Peter boldly proclaimed, "Even if all fall away on account of you, I never will" (verse 33). He went on to boast, "Even if I have to die with you, I will never disown you" (verse 35).

What did Peter do? In a moment of weakness, he

betrayed Jesus. He denied he even knew Jesus, not just once, not just twice, but three times. Immediately, after his third denial, Peter heard a rooster crow. "Then Peter remembered the word Jesus had spoken: 'Before the rooster crows, you will disown me three times.' And he went outside and wept bitterly" (verse 75). Peter's repentance was genuine and Jesus forgave him.

In contrast, Judas Iscariot betrayed Jesus but Judas was not forgiven. Why? He did not repent. He did not ask for forgiveness. Instead of shedding bitter tears in repentance, Judas committed suicide (Matthew 27:5 NIV).

Notice how our Lord Jesus, the offended party, dealt with a humble and repentant betrayer named Peter. Just four days after the betrayal the resurrected Lord Jesus asked Peter three times, once for each betrayal, "Do you truly love Me?" (John 21). Each time Peter said, "Yes, Lord; I love You."

It is not my purpose to digress into a lesson on the Greek words for love. However, I do want you to notice…Jesus never questioned Peter's sincerity. He never once said, "Peter, I warned you. You didn't listen to Me. I told you so." Instead, Jesus answered Peter's three affirmations of love with a reminder of Peter's assignment: "Feed my lambs" (verse 15), "Take care of my sheep" (verse 16), and "Feed my sheep" (verse 17). Jesus still had a purpose for Peter's life.

Jesus never mentioned Peter's betrayal. Not once. Why? Because when Jesus died on the cross and shed His blood for Peter's sins, He forgave them fully, finally, and forever. Jesus is always faithful to His promise: "If we confess our sins, he is faithful and just and will forgive us our sins and purify us from all unrighteousness" (1 John 1:9 NIV).

You remember the day your spouse promised to cleave unto you and you alone until death do you part. Now you know it did not happen. The promise was broken. Has he or she now asked your forgiveness? How will you respond? Does Jesus' response to Peter say anything to you?

Fifth, if you are the victim of adultery … don't fly off the handle and walk out. Take a moment to …

Reflect on Your Options

The news probably came like a punch in the stomach; your spouse violated your marriage bed. You were angry, humiliated, and maybe in denial. Now that you know it is true, how will you respond? I have seen three different responses over the years.

Some *freeze*. They refuse to face reality. Some wives are fairly confident their husbands are unfaithful—they've seen the lipstick, the makeup, and even found love notes— but they don't want to hear it. They choose to live in a state of denial.

Others *fold* like a cheap card table. They give up. Their immediate response to the news is, "Okay, it happened. The Bible says I can divorce you because you've been unfaithful. Our marriage is over. You are scum. Never touch me or come near me again. I don't want to talk to you. Counselling is out of the question. Let's just look in the Yellow Pages for a $99 divorce."

The third option is to *forgive*. You say, "How could I ever forgive him/her for what's been done to me?" My question for you is, "How could Jesus forgive you for what you've done to him?" Forgiveness is always an option.

The prophet Hosea was the victim of adultery. No doubt, every fiber of his being screamed, "*Get Out!*" But he heard the Lord say, "Go show your love to your wife again, though she has been loved by another and is an adulteress. Love her as the Lord loved the Israelites, though they turn to other gods" (Hosea 3:1 NIV). For Hosea, forgiveness wasn't an option; it was a mandate.

You may feel like you're incapable of forgiving. But Jesus isn't. I know of many couples who, with the Lord's help, have survived adultery and have gone on to have happy marriages for twenty, thirty, or forty years.

Ann Landers once received a letter from a woman who faced this conundrum. She had to choose whether she would freeze, fold, or forgive. Consider her thoughtful, well-reasoned decision. She wrote:

> Dear Ann,
>
> After 19 years of marriage I learned that my husband was committing adultery. I, too, demanded that he leave, but he refused to get out and begged forgiveness. Instead of going to hire a lawyer I asked myself some hard questions.
>
> 1) Would the children benefit emotionally and financially from a divorce? No, their lives would be disrupted. They would miss their father a great deal.
>
> 2) Would my career benefit from a divorce? No,

my job requires total concentration for 40 or 50 hours a week.

3) Would my husband's family, elderly parents, close siblings, benefit from a divorce? No, it would kill his mother. She believes him to be the perfect son, husband and father.

4) Do I want to change my lifestyle? No.

5) What is the bottom line regarding my feelings? Wounded pride because he preferred her to me.

6) Can I live with and recover from wounded pride? Yes, my husband and I talked at length. We agreed on two things: a) I would never mention his affair with the woman again. b) He would end the affair and never have another one.

It is five years later. We both have lived up to the agreement. It was not easy for me. I had to learn to put the other woman out of my mind. When we argued, it was about the matter at hand. I never bring up the past. I do not think about what if, where is he, will he again? He's a better husband than before; more caring, more compassionate. We value each other and all that we have. My pride? I have more self-esteem than ever, knowing I did the right thing and knowing I can face and conquer most anything that life can throw at me. I just received a promotion at work. Our children are happy and well adjusted. [And] his mother died last fall with a loving intact family at her bedside.

Signed,
Been There in D.C.

If you choose to forgive, I encourage you to ...

Reject Separation

Now is the time to act *rationally*, not rashly. When you married, God instructed you to *leave* and to *cleave*. You promised to stick together "for better or worse." This is one of those "worse" times.

Sometimes people say, "*Well, I just need to get away for a week or two.*" No, you don't. Now is the time the two of you most need to talk. You are extremely vulnerable. You feel futile and forsaken. Inevitably, during separation, the devil will slip an appealing person into your life. This person will seem to be everything your spouse isn't. He or she will give sympathy and extra attention that seems to anesthetize the deep wound in your heart. You will be more anxious to hear his/her voice than God's voice. Confusion is the last thing you need at this impressionable time.

Don't separate. Now is the time to develop a bond that will endure through thick and thin. When you are going through the aftermath of an affair, even if you are fighting, stay together.

Then seventh ...

Reach Out for Help

"Listen to advice and accept instruction, and in the end you will be wise" (Proverbs 19:20).

You won't like to hear this, but I'll tell you because I'm your friend. It will probably take months—maybe years—to put your marriage back together. And you're going to need help.

Choose a counselor known for helping couples rebuild their marriages. But beware. Counselors are not all created equal. Some become discouraged when a marriage doesn't heal quickly. They may recommend divorce, just when you are on the verge of a breakthrough. Reach out for help, but reach for help wisely.

Think It Through

The problem of adultery is evident. No one is immune. Good intentions will not protect you. The enemy is working against you. The devil uses seven destructive tools to demolish marriages. But thank God, there is hope!

The prescription for healing adultery is available. You can take it even if you are already infected. You can repent and confess your sin. You can run from the illicit relationship and resolve to avoid all future contact. Humble yourself to God and your spouse and request forgiveness. If you are the wronged spouse, reflect on your options. Reject separation and reach out for help. The prescription may be bitter going down, but the results will be rewarding.

Both of you can rely on God's power and grace. One of you needs the power to repent. The other needs the grace to forgive. Power and grace are available in Jesus Christ. Will you surrender yourself and your marriage to his Lordship?

Keeping Beauty

The moment you dreamed of has finally arrived. It is surreal.

You wipe the perspiration from your brow with a clean handkerchief. The stylus is in your trembling hand and you are prepared to write.

The category is "literature." You made your wager. Alex Trebek begins reading the Final Jeopardy challenge. "This French writer studied law and worked in government service during the days of King Louis XIV. He is credited with originating the 'fairy tale' literary genre. *Sleeping Beauty* is one of his best loved fairy tales."

The familiar music begins, "Dum di dum dum, dum di dum..." Your heart is racing; you can hardly believe your ears. You actually know the answer if you can just move your hand. Finally, your brain shifts into gear and convinces your hand to write the winning answer: "Who is Charles Perrault?"

If you actually knew the answer, then you are probably aware that Perrault's original story has been updated and softened through the years. The Brothers Grimm changed the ending and added our favorite line, "They lived happily ever after," except they wrote, "They lived contented to the end of their days." Tchaikovsky made it a ballet. And of course, Walt Disney added the dancing squirrels, rabbits, and birds.

In Perrault's story, Sleeping Beauty, her dog, all the servants in her father's castle, and even the flies on the kitchen wall slept for 100 years. She is called Sleeping Beauty because her beauty did not fade. She awoke 100 years later looking as ravishing as the day she went to sleep. And that's why it's called a fairy tale.

Age advances mercilessly. No one is exempt. Physical beauty fades.

Thankfully, relationships don't have to fade. You can keep the beauty in your marriage. In fact, the relationship between a husband and wife can grow more and more beautiful with each passing year. It won't happen automatically or by accident; love grows and deepens only where it is cultivated. You can take specific actions to focus your heart on your spouse.

Every marriage is unique because it is the combination of two unique personalities. You are made in God's image; and the Creator made you creative. Therefore, you can discover uniquely creative ways to keep the beauty in your relationship. Some of these may be personal and private just between the two of you. But allow me to stir your creative fires with seven action steps you can take to keep the beauty in your marriage. First…

Regulate Your Thoughts

Your thoughts are a significant part of the foundation on which you build both successes and failures. It is true in business. The multi-million bestseller, *Think and Grow Rich*, focuses on that single point. It's true for your lifestyle. Your thoughts determine whether you live a healthy or unhealthy lifestyle. And it is especially true for your marriage. That's because your actions follow your thoughts.

Solomon said, "For as he thinks in his heart, so *is* he" (Proverbs 23:7, NKJV). In other words, you become what you think. Of course, the word "think" does not refer to a passing thought. Fortunately, you don't act on every thought. But you do act on your considered, calculated thoughts. The Hebrew word pictures a person calculating the monetary value of something.[1] It refers to focused, thoughtful meditation. Actions grow out of such thinking. You can focus on thinking loving thoughts about your spouse and it will lead to loving actions toward your spouse.

God commands husbands to love their wives in the same way Jesus Christ loves his church (Ephesians 5:25 NIV). I am to love Dawn and you are to love your spouse with a self-sacrificing love. God commands wives to respect their husbands (verse 33). Dawn is to respect me and you are to respect your spouse just like Sarah respected Abraham (1 Peter 3:1–6 NIV).

Now some married people will protest by saying, "That's

a tall order. I don't feel love or respect for my spouse. If I don't feel it, how can I think loving or respectful thoughts?"

The answer is simple, but the accomplishment presents a greater challenge. It is a simple fact that feelings follow actions. Thinking and acting will lead to feeling. You don't wait until you feel like responding to a work-related problem. You tackle it head on. You know the good feeling will come after you've solved the problem. Marriage works the same way. Feelings follow actions.

If you do not feel loving toward your spouse, it is a sure sign you are not acting in a loving way. If you are not acting in a loving way, it is a sure sign you are not thinking loving thoughts. So regulate your thoughts.

A couple usually loses romantic feelings for one another long before a divorce. In fact, they likely think the loss of feelings justifies the divorce. One Christian sociologist gives the assurance that romantic feelings can be restored if a husband and wife are willing to do the work. He recommends that a couple make a thirty-day commitment. The husband and wife must commit to treating each other the way they treated one another when they had great romantic feelings. They have to act toward one another as they did when they were courting. The writer states:

His job is to tell her how beautiful she is, buy her flowers, take her out to dinner, and so on—in short, to do all the things that he did when he was "in love" with her. She has the same assignment, to treat her husband like a new boyfriend. Tell him how handsome he is, cook his favorite meal.... For those couples committed enough to go through that difficult assignment, the feelings always return.... The feelings will follow the actions.[2]

It all begins with regulating your thoughts. Thoughts lead to actions, and actions lead to feelings.

Popular culture says, "You can't control your heart. You can't choose whom you will love." Well of course you can! Regulate your thoughts toward your spouse, choose to act accordingly, and your feelings will follow.

Adultery is a prime example. Culture assumes your heart may lead you into an affair, and if it does, you can't do anything about it. Some suggest you shouldn't even try. But Jesus corrects the culture. He says "that anyone who looks at a woman lustfully has already committed adultery with her in his heart" (Matthew 5:27 NIV). Your "heart" is not your blood pump, but your thought process—the center of your thinking, reasoning, decision making, as well as your emotions, will, and whole inner being.[3] You will avoid adultery if you regulate your thoughts.

Remember: When you said, "I do" at the marriage altar, you gave up the right to think about another person in a romantic way. You forfeited the right to flirt with anyone but your spouse.

When an attractive person crosses your path and you are tempted to lust... choose to pray for the person instead. Remember that she is somebody else's daughter, sister, wife, mother... and she does not belong to you.

Remember that he is someone else's son, brother, husband, father … and he does not belong to you.

Regulate your thoughts. It will keep the beauty in your marriage. Second …

Restrict Your Eyes

This suggestion is especially vital for men who want to keep the beauty in their relationship. King David learned this lesson the hard way. His eyes got him into trouble with Bathsheba. His unrestricted gaze produced unregulated thoughts, and the thoughts led to rebellious actions. He committed adultery (2 Samuel 11 NIV).

After his repentance David resolved, "I will set before my eyes no vile thing" (Psalm 101:3 NIV). His son Solomon noted the wisdom of both regulating your thoughts and restricting your eyes. He wrote, "Above all else, guard your heart, for it is the wellspring of life … Let your eyes look straight ahead, fix your gaze directly before you" (Proverbs 4:23, 25 NIV).

Restricting your eyes is an important attitude and action that will help you keep the beauty in your marriage. Your spouse is keenly aware of where you look and who has your attention. When you stare at another person in interest, your spouse may pretend not to notice, but your glances are like daggers in the heart. Staring with interest at another attractive person is high treason in marriage. Your spouse has the right to expect your eyes and heart to sing in harmony, "I only have eyes for you." Restrict your eyes. Third …

Reduce Your Temptations

Jesus said, "The spirit is willing, but the body is weak" (Matthew 26:41 NIV). That's why it is vital to reduce temptations.

- If your DVDs tempt you to think ungodly thoughts, break them.

- If the hotel TV beckons you to watch porn … have the hotel personnel disconnect it.

- If a sexy secretary is a temptation, transfer her to another department.

- If the *Cosmopolitan* magazine tempts you, burn it and cancel the subscription.

- If your neighbor mows her lawn in a bikini, pull down the shades.

"Clothe yourselves with the Lord Jesus Christ, and do not think about how to gratify the desires of the sinful nature" (Romans 13:14 NIV). Notice the *New King James* translation of the same verse. "Put on the Lord Jesus Christ, and make no provision for the flesh, to fulfill its lusts." Comparing the two translations brings out the meaning. When you have a sinful desire, don't give it calculated thought. Don't expect God to give you victory over a sin if you are gathering the needed supplies and developing a strategy for how you will commit the sin.

Remember, thoughts lead to actions and actions lead to feelings. The sinful thoughts, actions, and feelings will distract you from seeing and enjoying the beauty in your marriage. So, reduce your temptations.

God does not want you to see how close you can get to the precipice of sin without falling over. The initial slip may give you a momentary feeling of exhilaration, but the sudden crash will be a disaster.

Help yourself. Regulate your thoughts, restrict your eyes, and reduce your temptations. Fourth…

Resolve to Meet Your Spouse's Needs

Any of your spouse's needs that you are not currently fulfilling is an Achilles heel in your marriage. You are vulnerable there.

Your spouse has emotional and social needs. Your spouse needs acceptance and love. Your spouse has physical and sexual needs. Resolve to meet those needs.

Men and women are different. Aren't you glad! Generally speaking, men and women have dramatically different needs. God made us that way. A man has a profound need to know his wife respects him. He needs to know his wife looks up to him as the leader of their home. He needs to know she trusts and depends on him as a man. A woman has a deep inner need to know she is loved unconditionally. She needs to know she can trust her husband and be secure in their relationship. That's why God inspired Paul to write:

> Wives, *submit* to your husbands as to the Lord.… Husbands, *love* your wives, just as Christ *loved* the church and gave himself up for her.… In this same way, husbands ought to *love* their wives as their own

bodies. He who *loves* his wife *loves* himself. After all, no one ever hated his own body, but he feeds and cares for it, just as Christ does the church.... However, each one of you also must *love* his wife as he loves himself, and the wife must *respect* her husband.

Ephesians 5:22, 25, 28–29, 33 (NIV)

Ladies, physical intimacy is vital for men. I've counselled men whose wives had not been physically affectionate for months—in some cases, *years*. To be sure, the lack of physical intimacy does not excuse him to have an affair. But it does make him vulnerable to an affair. That's why the Bible says to married couples, "Do not deprive each other except by mutual consent and for a time, so that you may devote yourselves to prayer. Then come together again so that Satan will not tempt you because of your lack of self-control" (1 Corinthians 7:5 NIV).

Sexual intimacy between a husband and wife, as God intends it, is much more than a physical act. It is also psychologically fulfilling. When a husband and wife freely and joyfully give themselves to one another, the husband communicates unconditional love and acceptance. He's saying, "Even after all these years, you are still my bride, my sweetheart. You please and fulfill me just as you are. No one else in the world is worthy of intruding into our private, intimate world." The wife who freely gives herself to her husband communicates trust, respect, and joy in her husband. She frees and inspires him emotionally to be the man God intends him to be.

Your marital intimacy is also a spiritual issue. The husband and wife who understand and meet one another's needs deepen their intimacy with God and have their prayers answered. "Wives, in the same way be submissive to your husbands...Husbands, in the same way be considerate as you live with your wives, and treat them with respect as the weaker partner and as heirs with you of the gracious gift of life, so that nothing will hinder your prayers" (1 Peter 3:1, 7 NIV).

Therefore, the husband and wife who want to keep the beauty in their marriage must resolve to meet their spouse's needs. Fifth...

Refuse Isolation

I hope you are seeing how one suggestion builds on another. If you regulate your thoughts, restrict your eyes, reduce your temptations, and resolve to meet your spouse's needs, you will readily refuse isolation. Of course, isolation does not refer to time alone with God. Both of you need that; you must have it.

The isolation I am urging you to refuse is the stereotypical, emotionally isolated and distant executive. Everyone sees him as personable, outgoing, and successful. Everyone, that is, except his wife and children. To them, he is moody and distant. He comes home exhausted. He is in the house without being at home. All his energy has been invested in the company. Nothing is left for his wife and children. He is far more attentive to the needs of his employees than to the needs of his family. As he climbs the corporate ladder, the distance between him and his wife grows proportionately.

A wife can become equally isolated from her husband. She can isolate herself in her career or even in their children. She can pour so much energy into being supermom that she has no time or energy or interest in her husband. Clearly, the husband and wife who want to keep the beauty in their marriage will refuse isolation.

Retirement often magnifies rather than cures the problem. In my pastorate near Tampa, Florida, I see thousands of newly retired couples. Some drive into town miles apart in the same Cadillac or Mercedes. They have spent years carefully investing and saving and preparing to live comfortably through this stage of their lives. But they failed to invest any time in building their marriage. Plush retirement homes, swimming pools, sunshine, and palm trees cannot bridge the gap between isolated couples.

One Bible example will help explain. Isolation made King David vulnerable to temptation. He was at the height of his career. He had acquired everything money could buy. His people loved and honored him, God's supernatural favour was upon him, and even his enemies respected him. Yet, as his power and popularity increased, so did his isolation. No one held King David accountable. The Bible describes his isolation.

> In the spring, at the time when kings go off to war, David sent Joab out with the king's men and the whole Israelite army.... But David remained in Jerusalem.

> One evening David got up from his bed and
> walked around on the roof of the palace. From the
> roof he saw a woman bathing. The woman was
> very beautiful…Then David sent messengers to
> get her. She came to him, and he slept with her.
>
> 2 Samuel 11:1–2, 4 (NIV)

King David was isolated and unaccountable. It was a recipe for disaster for David and it will be for you as well. Dear friend, don't allow yourself to be isolated for long periods. Be accountable. For you, accountability may mean putting your computer in the family room, and only using the Internet when others can monitor you. Accountability may mean finding an accountability partner who will ask you the tough questions. When you are on a business trip, maybe your accountability partner will call your hotel room at unexpected times and ask what you are watching on television, reading, or viewing on the web. Accountability may mean letting your secretary know where you are at all times during the day. Whatever it takes for you, be accountable.

Refusing isolation will help you keep the beauty in your marriage, even in retirement. You can be sure a deadly distance does not grow between you and your spouse. Sixth…

Recognize "Electricity"

Those who faithfully regulate their thoughts, restrict their eyes, reduce their temptations, resolve to meet their spouse's needs, and refuse isolation will enjoy a renewed "electricity" in their marriage. That's great. That's what God intends. It will help you keep the beauty in your relationship.

Problems arise, however, when you begin to relish the "electricity" between you and someone other than your spouse. Before working on the electrical system in your home an electrician will turn off the power, then use a voltage meter to be sure no power remains in the wires. Electricians have a healthy respect for electricity.

You, likewise, must have a healthy respect for "electricity" between you and another person. Turn up the voltage between you and your spouse. Turn off the voltage between you and anyone else. "But among you there must not be even a hint of sexual immorality, or of any kind of impurity, or of greed, because these are improper for God's holy people" (Ephesians 5:3 NIV).

Notice the word "hint." The moment you sense an electrical buzz between you and someone of the opposite sex, the moment you begin to think about being with that person, get out of there. *Flee!* Don't wait until an acquaintance becomes a friend who becomes an intimate friend who becomes a lover.

Some teenagers from broken homes were in a group counseling session. An Attractive teen-age girl was asked about her daddy who had been a pastor. The counselor asked, "Can you describe what it was like when your daddy told your family he was leaving your mother?" she said. "It was just like he walked into our family room with a ticking bomb, rolled it into the middle of our family circle, and then walked out, leaving us to deal with the explosion."

The risk is too great. Too much is at stake. Recognize electricity. Seventh...

Reflect on the Consequences

Do you long for the kind of marriage that's been described in this chapter? The consequences for keeping beauty in your marriage are well worth your focused attention. It is a priority investment; it will pay rewarding dividends. On the other hand, the consequences of not regulating your thoughts, restricting your eyes, reducing your temptations, resolving to meet your spouse's needs, refusing isolation, and recognizing electricity will be deadly for your marriage.

A game warden in northern Michigan stopped a man carrying two buckets of Walleye fish away from a lake. The Game Warden asked, "Do you have a license to catch those fish?"

"No, sir," the man replied. "I wasn't fishing. These are my pet fish."

"Pet fish?!"

"Yes, sir. Every night I take these fish down to the lake and let them swim around. It's good exercise and they seem to enjoy it. After a while I whistle, they jump back into the buckets, and I take them home."

The game warden was incensed. "That's a bunch of hooey! Fish can't do that."

The man looked at the game warden for a moment and then said, "Here, I'll show you."

"Okay. I've got to see this." The game warden was curious now.

The man poured the fish into the lake, stood, and waited. After several minutes of both men staring across the water, the man said, "It's a pleasant evening, isn't it?"

"Well?" asked the game warden.

"Well, what?" asked the man.

"When are you going to call them back?"

"Call who back?" the man asked.

"The *fish*."

"What fish?" the man asked.

At this point, the game warden realized he had been tricked but the deed had been done.

Problems do not go away if you ignore or deny them. You might hide the evidence for a while, but it will resurface somewhere. Intentional action is required to keep the beauty in your marriage.

I have a friend who is a marriage counselor. When he counsels a couple contemplating divorce, he leads them through a little exercise. He asks, "Do you think your marriage of ten (twenty... thirty...) years is important enough for you to spend thirty minutes a day for six days, seeking a reconciliation? Is your marriage worth three hours of your time?" If they agree, he gives the following assignment.

He instructs them to divide the daily thirty-minute session into six, five-minute segments. *The first five minutes: Sit together and think about your future for five minutes, without either of you saying a word.* What will your future be like by yourself?

He says to the wife, "Think about all the friends you've had together. You are going to lose 90% of them. Think about rearing your children alone, without a father. What impact will these things have on you?"

To the husband he says, "Think about the alimony the court will require you to pay. Think about the loneliness. Think about only seeing your children every other Saturday. Just think about these realities for the first five minutes."

The next five minutes: Think about yourself. Ask yourself, "Have I played a part in this divorce? Did I have any part in the sin that's destroying our marriage?" Think about yourself, your role, your inadequacy, and your sins of commission and sins of omission. Just think about yourself for five minutes.

The third five minutes: Think about your children. How will your kids be scarred and devastated by this divorce? Don't fool yourself. None are exempt. Divorce scars every child.

In the first fifteen minutes, say nothing to each other. That shouldn't be hard. You probably haven't communicated much in months anyway. The next fifteen minutes, however, may be a little more challenging.

The fourth five minutes: Open your Bible to 1 Corinthians 13:4–8. Let the wife read the verses the first day. Let the husband read them the second day. Go right through those five verses, reading in turn for six days. Seek to understand God's definition of love.

Love is patient, love is kind. It does not envy, it does not boast, it is not proud. It is not rude, it is not self-seeking, it is not easily angered, it keeps no record of wrongs. Love does not delight in evil but rejoices with the truth. It always protects, always trusts, always hopes, always perseveres. Love never fails.

1 Corinthians 13 (NIV)

Talk about ways you can express God's kind of love to one another. So far, you have invested twenty minutes in saving your marriage.

The fifth five minutes: Play the "Do you remember?" game. Remember positive times in your marriage. Go back to the day you walked on the beach holding hands as the sun went down and the waves rolled in. Go back to the night you stayed up together all night, praying over your sick child. Go back to that moment when one of you experienced a great tragedy and your spouse was there to love and encourage you. Go back to that moment when you were trying to furnish your first apartment. Go back to the funny moments, the hilarious moments, the tearful moments, and the joyful moments, the times you had fun together and valued one another. Finally . . .

The sixth five minutes: Focus on one verse, Psalm 46:10, and pray. The verse says, "Be still and know that I am God." Both of you pray aloud, *"Oh, Lord, this is what I think went wrong in our marriage. Help us."*

How is your marriage? Have you kept the beauty in your relationship? If not, you probably feel the "electricity" was turned off long ago. You may feel your marriage is beyond human help and hope. However, I do not believe it is beyond God. The consequences of giving up will be huge.

Would you invest thirty minutes a day for six days to save your marriage? Would you be willing for God to restore your marriage if He could? Do you have the courage to "be still," to take your hands off the controls, and see what God can do? Will you together, give your marriage to God?

Incorporate the seven suggested attitudes and actions into your marriage, and I am convinced you will see the beauty restored. Regulate Your Thoughts. Restrict Your Eyes. Reduce Your Temptations. Resolve to Meet Your Spouse's Needs. Refuse Isolation. Recognize "Electricity." Reflect On the Consequences.

A Storybook Marriage is not automatic, but it is available. It is available to those who focus on Keeping Beauty.

Afterword

A Storybook Testimony

Throughout *A Storybook Marriage* I have shown that God's great purpose and good intentions for your marriage are not fulfilled by accident. You must be intentional about growing your marriage. Unless relationships are nurtured, entropy sets in. Like a vegetable garden, love flourishes when the right seeds are planted and faithfully cultivated. Otherwise, weeds take over. Perhaps you feel your marriage garden is hopelessly overgrown. You've waited too long. Cultivation seems to be out of the question.

Allow me one final chance to offer you hope. A friend's testimony may help. It weaves multiple principles that we have reviewed into one story. Read it; then I will connect the dots.

When Judy and I married, June 4, 1976, we had known one another for nine marvelous months. We were confident we would have the first perfect marriage since Adam and Eve. If *A Storybook Marriage* had been written at the time, we would have expected our picture to be on the front cover.

Our compatibility was easy to recognize. Our backgrounds were compatible. We were both raised in the homes of Bible-believing Baptist pastors. Our faith was compatible. Both of us received Jesus Christ as our Lord and Savior when we were children. Both of us were baptized, active members of the same church. We both read the Bible and prayed every day, and we both were praying for God to bring His chosen spouse into our lives. Our education was compatible. We met at a Christian college in Chattanooga, Tennessee, as seniors. Our life goals were even compatible. God had called me to be a pastor. God had called Judy to be a pastor's wife. What better start could a couple have?

We were certain God had brought us together and that we were deeply in love. We had both taken a college class called "Courtship and Marriage." Furthermore, we had both read several books about marriage. We were under the delusion that we were matrimonial experts. Then we got married. As Pastor Forrest says, "Like twirling a baton or eating with chopsticks, marriage is easy until you try it."

The first six months of our acquaintance, we were both in college. We went to school in the morning, Judy had a second shift job, and I had a third shift job.

I proposed after we had dated for three months. Our dates centered around three activities. We met in the college Dining Hall for breakfast and lunch every day. A couple of times a week we sat and talked in the living room of her parents' apartment, and we sat together at church on Sunday and Wednesday night. Obviously, I was the last of the big spenders!

I finished college a semester before Judy, and moved to Memphis, Tennessee, to begin seminary. Consequently, the last three months before our wedding, we saw each other a total of nine days.

When we married, we had never had an argument or even disagreed about anything. We thought it was because we were so deeply in love and because we were such mature Christians. (We were both twenty-one years old.) Unfortunately, it turned out that we had just never spent enough time together. Our expectation of never having an argument ended on the third day of our marriage.

Even so, things were good for the first three years. We lived eighty miles outside of Memphis where I was the pastor of a small country church. As a full-time seminary student, I commuted to seminary four days a week (640 miles per week). I usually left at 6:00 a.m. and returned by 6:00 p.m. after having made hospital visits on the way home. With studying for school, sermon preparation, and church visitation, I was seldom home much more than to eat one meal a day and sleep five or six hours.

Five days after I graduated from seminary, we moved to Indiana to plant a new church. By that time we had a beautiful one-year-old daughter. A handsome baby boy was added to our family ten months later.

Our new church plant had no building, so my office

was at home. For the first time in our married life I was around all the time. To our great shock, we discovered we didn't like each other very much. Of course we didn't realize this right away. It was a growing revelation as we gradually discovered one another's irritating habits and idiosyncrasies (By the way, everyone has some). Whether your spouses' habits are irritating or endearing depends on your attitude. Unfortunately, Judy and I often chose irritation over endearment.

Our life had many stresses. We had ministry stresses. What church doesn't? We had financial stresses, and family stresses. What young family with a small income and two preschoolers doesn't? Instead of turning to one another for strength and comfort, we turned on one another to vent our frustrations. In private, our relationship increasingly was dominated by bickering. We waged an ongoing campaign of verbal attacks and counter-attacks.

The bickering periodically escalated into an all out screaming argument. After a volcanic eruption we would apologize and try to get along for a while. But it never lasted. After my multiple apologies for the same offense, Judy said, "You say you're sorry, but you don't mean it. You don't change anything."

Publicly, we put on a good front. Most people thought we were an exemplary young Christian family with two cute little blond children. We looked like we had it all together.

Now please understand: we weren't trying to be deceptive. We were just trying to manage life. Airing our dirty laundry in public certainly would not have helped. I don't recommend that you air any of your dirty laundry in public either.

A dear lady in our new church had lost a son who would have been about my age. Perhaps her motherly instincts clouded her perception of reality, but she thought I was a grand young preacher with great potential. One Sunday after a service she said to Judy, "It must be wonderful being married to Tim." Judy tried to smile, and answered, "Oh, you just can't imagine."

As our fifth anniversary approached, I realized more and more that I was miserable. We weren't *companions*. We were combatants. We didn't try to solve problems; we only tried to win arguments. We had very little good *communication*. The only thing we had was a *commitment* to the *permanence* of marriage.

Divorce wasn't an option for us. We believed God's meant it when He said, "I hate divorce" (Malachi 2:16). I knew abandoning our marriage would be abandoning my call to ministry. This is shameful to admit, but I began to think, "How can I endure being married to this dud for the next fifty years?" Down in the depths of my wicked heart, I sometimes wished Judy would die. I didn't want her to have a slow lingering death, leaving me with a big hospital bill. I didn't hate her; I didn't want her to suffer. I just wanted her to go quickly and painlessly in her sleep. Then, I thought, I could use my two cute little children as bait for a good wife.

Things finally came to a head a couple of months before our sixth anniversary. Our mutual misery forced us to be honest with ourselves and with one another.

Late one night, sitting on our bed, we faced the fact that we had serious problems and we didn't want to go on as we were. We both confessed, "I love you, but I don't like you." We both confessed, "Sometimes I think you would be better off without me." Judy cried a lot. I felt ashamed.

We agreed we wanted our relationship to be right, but we needed a miracle. We needed God's supernatural intervention.

Fortunately we did not decide to wait and see what would happen. We determined to be proactive. We agreed to go into separate rooms and write a list of all the things we didn't like about one another. We then exchanged and read one another's lists. Instead of denying our faults, we acknowledged our guilt. We apologized for being hard to live with, agreed on a few specific things we could and would change, and threw away the lists. Holding on to them would have been neither loving nor forgiving. "Love … keeps no record of wrongs" (1 Cor. 13:5).

We then joined hands and prayed for a miracle. We asked God to forgive our sinful attitudes, empower us to change, and enable us to like one another again. With that serious, simple, humble, and honest prayer, there was an immediate change within us. God graciously intervened. The wall between us began to crumble.

Finally, we followed through on our promises. The very next morning we began making the specific changes we had promised to make. And our relationship started a gradual process of improvement.

One day, a few months later, it occurred to me that I really liked Judy. I honestly enjoyed her company. I no longer wanted her to die. I discovered I was already married to the good wife I had hoped to find.

More than a quarter of a century has gone by since that memorable night, and we are still building on the new foundation. Life has continued to present challenges. We have gone from being parents of preschoolers to being grandparents of preschoolers. We still aren't perfect. I'm still pretty hard to live with at times. But we are learning to make periodic course adjustments. We continue growing together. We continue to cultivate the garden of our marriage.

Today I can honestly say that the greatest joy and strength in my life, other than Jesus Christ, continues to be my wife. We are writing a new chapter of our *Storybook Marriage*.

Marriage can be a storybook or nightmare. A storybook marriage requires *companionship, cooperation, communication,* and *commitment*, along with a large dose of forgiveness, grace, and the power of God.

Now let me quickly connect some of the dots. Tim and Judy's marriage was in trouble. Unknowingly, they were following a destructive path. They were violating all seven of the "Laws of Longevity" (Chapter 2). They were a classic example of the "Dumbo" mistake of "Being Reckless with Words" (Chapter 3). They had "Ruined Romance" and were moving quickly and carelessly through the "Four Stages of Heart Hurt" (Chapter 4). Fortunately, they were committed to "The Permanence Of Marriage" (Chapter 2). God led them through the four steps to "Reignite Romance" (Chapter 4); their marriage was restored and their family and ministry were saved.

If you are considering a divorce, please don't. The good

husband or wife you are seeking is already living with you. You just need God's supernatural intervention and a mutual commitment to change what needs to be changed.

Would you be willing for God to save your marriage? Even if you think you can't change, would you be willing to be changed? Approach your marriage in God's way, and a new storybook can begin. And you might just live happily ever after.

Epilogue

Just weeks after my husband finished writing this book, my greatest fear became my reality. My husband, Forrest Pollock, and my son, Preston, were involved in an airplane crash.

Now, every morning I have a choice to make ... "Should I stay in bed because I have no strength to move on and allow life's circumstances to get me down or should I get up and live for Christ?" I know I owe it to my other five kids to test and prove that in the valley of death, the faith that their daddy and Preston had and the faith we profess, is to be trusted, relied upon, lived and believed.

Sometimes life doesn't make sense and we don't understand. But when I say, "I can't!" God says, "He can through me." When I feel like I can't go on, I've learned to say, "Now that I am here, in my life Lord, what next?" We will continue to live our lives for the Lord and look forward to being reunited with them in Heaven.

This book was finished in honor of my husband and our Storybook Marriage, and for my son, Preston.

Resting in His love,

L. Dawn Pollock

Endnotes

Chapter 1

1. Read God's promises to Abraham in Genesis 12:1–3 and 15:1–6.

2. Kenneth A. Mathews, *Genesis 11:27–50:26* in *The New American Commentary*, vol. 1b, gen. ed. E. Ray Clendenen (Nashville: Broadman & Holman, 2005), 326. Mathews states, "The importance of the assignment is heightened by the stature of the servant Abraham selected; he is the senior administrator... of the entire household (v. 2). Also the patriarch imposes an oath on the servant, requiring the sign of placing his hand on Abraham's thigh. The same rite occurs when aged Jacob implores Joseph to bury him in Canaan (47:29). The thigh indicates the procreative power and heritage of the patriarch's position as the source of the family."

3. Catherine C. Harris, "Creature of the Desert, Camel" (accessed 18 September 2007); available from http://www.touregypt.net/featurestories/camel.htm.

Chapter 2

1. "English Channel" (accessed 12 October 2007); available from http://en.wikipedia.org/wiki/English_Channel.

2. ²"Dolley Payne Todd Madison" (accessed 19 October 2007); available from http://www.whitehouse.gov/history/firstladies/dm4.html.

Chapter 3

1. Genesis 2:24; Matthew 19:5; Mark 10:7; Ephesians 5:31.

2. A full, readable, and from my perspective, Biblical discussion of this issue can be found in Wayne Grudem, *Evangelical Feminism: A New Path to Liberalism?* (Wheaton: Crossway Books, 2006).

Chapter 4

1. Tim LaHaye and Jerry B. Jenkins, *John's Story: The Last Eyewitness* (New York: Putnam Praise, 2006), 3–22.

2. The survey was conducted by Kelton Research, an independent firm.

3. "What are the most common Causes for Divorce?"

(accessed 06 December 2007); available from http://www.divorcereform.org/cau.html.

Chapter 5

1. Notice the various warnings in Proverbs 5:1–23; 6:20–35; 7:1–27.

2. *Mounce's Complete Expository Dictionary of Old and New Testament Words*, s.v., "adultery."

3. *Webster's Seventh New Collegiate Dictionary*, s.v., "adulterate."

4. Special thanks to Rick Warren for this outline.

5. "Midlife Crisis, Stress and Depression" (accessed 19 December, 2007); available from http://www.teamtechnology.co.uk/tt/t-articl/midlife.htm.

6. Charles H. Spurgeon, *The Treasury of David*, vol. 2, part 2 (McLean, VA: MacDonald Publishing Co., n.d.), 2:65.

Chapter 6

1. William D. Mounce, gen. ed., *Mounce's Complete Expository Dictionary of Old and New Testament Words* (Grand Rapids: Zondervan, 2006), s.v., "Think."

2. James C. Hunter, *The Servant* (New York: Crown Business, 1998), 150–151.

3. Mounce, s.v., "heart."